Jesus

For David

Luke 8:16

Jesus

Amy Welborn

Our Sunday Visitor Publishing Division
Our Sunday Visitor, Inc.
Huntington, Indiana 46750

Nihil Obstat
Rev. Michael Heintz
Censor Librorum

Imprimatur
✠ John M. D'Arcy
Bishop of Fort Wayne-South Bend
August 2, 2002

The Scripture citations used in this work are taken from the *New American Bible with Revised New Testament and Psalms,* copyright © 1991, 1986, 1970 by the Confraternity of Christian Doctrine, Inc., Washington, D.C. Used with permission. All rights reserved. No part of the *New American Bible* may be reproduced by any means without permission in writing from the copyright owner. Excerpts from the English translation of the *Catechism of the Catholic Church, Second Edition,* for use in the United States of America, copyright © 1994 and 1997, United States Catholic Conference – Libreria Editrice Vaticana. Used with permission. The author and publisher are grateful to those publishers and others whose materials, whether in the public domain or protected by copyright laws, have been used in one form or another in this volume. Every reasonable effort has been made to determine copyright holders of excerpted materials and to secure permissions as needed. If any copyrighted materials have been inadvertently used in this work without proper credit being given in one form or another, please notify Our Sunday Visitor in writing so that future printings of this work may be corrected accordingly.

ISBN: 978-087973-395-7 (Inventory No. 395)
LCCN: 2002107145

Cover design by Tyler Ottinger
Cover photo by John Zierten
Interior design by Sherri L. Hoffman
Interior illustrations by James Douglas Adams

PRINTED IN THE UNITED STATES OF AMERICA

Contents

Introduction

JESUS.

It's a name that's echoed in your consciousness forever, a name at the center of stories, prayers, art, music, and lots of wise sayings. A name connected to a man who did amazing things. A name that evokes all sorts of inspiring, comforting, sad, and hopeful thoughts, all jumbled together.

Jesus.

It's the name of the most important person who ever lived on earth. Ironic, isn't it? In this world that celebrates wealth, power, and military might, the most universally well-known figure died a criminal's death two thousand years ago, abandoned by almost all His friends.

Jesus.

WHEN YOU WERE LITTLE, you probably didn't have many problems with Jesus, and when you did, your questions were pretty simple, as were the answers you got.

If you happened to wonder, in the middle of dinner, how Jesus turned water into wine, the answer, "He could do that because He was God," probably satisfied you, and your mind moved on to the next challenge — how to toss that glob of mashed potatoes at your sister without being caught, maybe.

But things are different now. (You're not *still* throwing potatoes at your sister, are you? Well . . . *most* things are different, anyway.)

The world's a lot more complex than it was when you were five, and your brain practically bursts with questions about puzzles, ambiguities, and contradictions that wouldn't even have occurred to you way back then, when you received every statement from your parents' and teachers' lips as if their words were little gold nuggets of infallible truth.

So now you can't help but wonder: It's easy to *say* Jesus is God, but how did that work in real life? If He was God, why did He pray? How in the world could the Creator of the universe become a helpless and dependent human baby? How did that happen, exactly?

Your world's also a lot bigger now than it used to be. Back when you were small, all you knew was your own faith, your own church, and your own religion class. It was a cozy little place, defined by Froot Loops in the morning and a kiss and a hug good night. But everything — except maybe the Froot Loops — is different now.

You know there are literally billions of people around the world who don't believe Jesus is God, who worship other gods or no gods at all. You've even heard that a lot of what Jesus taught is echoed in other religions — stuff about loving your neighbor and putting your own concerns last. It makes you wonder whether Jesus is really so special, if He's really unique, if He's not just one of many wise teachers, and if you need to worry about Him at all.

Then, to be honest, there's Santa Claus.

And the Easter Bunny. And the Tooth Fairy.

All figures about which you were told stories when you were little. All nice little tales about fanciful beings who cared about you and would reward you if you were good.

You hate to admit it, and you really don't even want to think it, but to tell the truth, you can't help but wonder sometimes whether everything about God, including the whole Jesus business, falls into the same category. Could it be that the adults in your life told you all these stories about heaven and everything that leads up to it just to get you to behave yourself?

You don't welcome doubt, but the truth is, sometimes it simply descends on you like a big, sudden storm cloud.

While you're in the middle of that cloud, trying to see your way through the rain dripping down your glasses, you can't help but think that if a nonbeliever can be happy, what's the point, anyway?

So your questions expand, and just keep coming. You're not only asking how could Jesus do this or how could Jesus be that, but you're asking an even more fundamental question:

Why Jesus at all?

THOSE ARE THE QUESTIONS this book is going to try to help you answer. They're not easy questions, but you know, they're not impossible, either. In the two thousand years since the man named Jesus walked the earth, lots of people have spent hours, days, and even lifetimes trying to figure Him out, pondering the very same questions you have. So take comfort in knowing you're not alone, and you don't have to be in the dark, either. Way too often, we tend to think we can come up with answers to hard religious and philosophical questions just by sitting around in our room, turning the stereo up really loud, and staring at the ceiling.

It doesn't exactly work that way, though. It doesn't work with physics or algebra, and it doesn't work with religion, either. If you're serious about understanding Jesus, you have to go beyond the confines of what you already know and reach out to absorb what others can teach you.

Including Jesus Himself, of course.

Now, I'm really glad you're reading this book. I can't tell you how happy I am about that, and how much I hope you'll enjoy it and learn from it.

But I'm going to ask you to do something really strange here.

Right after you finish reading this introduction, and before you even turn the page to the next chapter, I want you to stop reading this book. Immediately.

And then, I want you to go find a Bible. We can all hope you don't have to even walk into the next room to find one, but if you do, or even if you have to pop down to the store and actually buy one, that's okay, too.

Just go get one, then open it up to the New Testament and find one of the Gospels. It doesn't matter which one, although it might be simpler if you started with one of what we call the Synoptic Gospels — Matthew, Mark, or Luke — and leave John, as wise and as wonderful as he is, for later.

Then start reading. Choose one of those Gospels and read every word of it, from the first to the last verse. It should only take you a few days or a couple of weeks, as none of the Gospels is terribly long. Just read through one and familiarize yourself with the events of Jesus' life as they're presented by people who were very, very close to the events. When you've finished, come back and see me again, and we can talk.

Here's why:

I can chat with you all day about what other people have said about Jesus, but none of it is going to make much sense to you unless you've taken the time and the effort to see what He has to say for Himself.

After all, you'd probably really hate it if someone judged you solely from what others said about you. You'd say that wasn't fair, that wasn't right, and there was no way anyone could really understand you if they depended on gossip and hearsay to figure you out.

> To be ignorant of the Scripture is not to know Christ.
>
> — St. Jerome, *In Isaiam*

It's the same with Jesus. You've heard about Him secondhand long enough. It's time to meet Him face-to-face.

I'm asking you to do that because I know why you're really here. You're not here just out of curiosity or some pursuit of abstract knowledge.

No, you're here because there are times, beyond all your questions and even doubts, when you look up at the wall of your room, or your classroom or church sanctuary, and you see the image of a man hanging there, nailed to a cross.

And try as you might, you can't take your eyes away from that image, and your heart and soul won't even let you.

You know that in that single amazing life and horrible death, lived and suffered hundreds of years ago, lies something that goes beyond a simple fact of history. You know that when you look at the image of that man, you feel something much different than you do when you run across a picture of George Washington or Cleopatra. You feel connected — not just from your end, but in this strange way, from His. This death, you know in your heart, has something to do with you, not because you want it to, but because *He* meant it to.

And you feel differently, not just because of what anyone has taught you or because of information you've absorbed in religion classes, but because of something that lives and breathes still.

It's hard for you to explain, but deep down, you know that what you experience when you look at that man on the cross is a voice. It's

a living voice that knows your name, loves you, and wants to embrace you in love and mercy.

Some people might be irritated by all your questions about that figure on the cross, and they might even tell you that your questions put your faith in danger. But you and I know that they don't.

We know that when you ask these questions, you're not looking for a way out of the love that voice promises. You're looking for a way to get in deeper, a way that makes sense, a way that you can talk about and relate to all that you know about the world, all that stuff you didn't know when you were five and one sentence was enough to answer all your questions.

So let's get started. The first step is up to you.

Do you have that Bible yet?

Go ahead. Open it up — and listen.

Here are some reliable Catholic editions of the Bible:

- *The Catholic Answer Bible* (Our Sunday Visitor)
- *The Ignatius Bible* (Ignatius Press)
- *The Holy Bible: New Revised Standard Version: Catholic Edition* (Oxford University Press)
- *The Catholic Bible: New American Bible/ Personal Study* (Oxford University Press)
- *The Jerusalem Bible: Reader's Edition* (Doubleday)

CHAPTER 1

PRETEND YOU'RE GOING ON A TRIP. Even better, pretend you're going on this particular trip by yourself, to a fantastic place you've never before visited, and best of all, you're driving.

You have a pretty great car, but it's not so fabulous that it has one of those on-board computer navigation systems that tell you exactly how many feet it is from your house to the mall. You, mere mortal that you are, must settle for a regular, old-fashioned, impossible-to-refold thing called a map.

Now, exactly what would be the most sensible attitude to have toward this map?

Would it make sense to decide that the mapmakers might have simply fabricated what you're holding in your hand from their imaginations?

Would it be reasonable to decide that what you have in your hand is nothing more than a clever ploy to steer you in the wrong direction, simply to benefit the mapmakers' own nefarious and greedy purposes?

Would it then be a good idea to determine that for these reasons (and any more that you can dream up), the map you have is useless and perhaps even dangerous, and you'd be better off stopping your car, standing on the hood, and deciding which way to go by what direction your hair is blowing?

I doubt it. You know that if you're going on this fabulous trip to a new place, you simply have to take a deep breath and trust that map.

It's not a blind trust, though. The trust you have in the map is rooted in your experience of how the world works — mapmakers would quickly go out of business if their maps routinely led people in the wrong direction. You also trust the map because people you know have trusted them before and done pretty well with them.

It's the same with this whole Jesus business. If you're serious about knowing Jesus, you can't just depend on what happens to be in your brain at the moment, your intuitions, or your emotions to arrive at that destination.

You have to trust the map.

So, what is the map we're talking about here?

It's the Gospels, of course. (Remember? You just read one of them, right?) By extension, because Jesus promised He'd always be with the Church as it helps the world understand the good news about Jesus, the map includes what the Church has taught about Jesus, too.

And just as it is with the map, the trust we have in Scripture and the Church to tell us the truth and lead us in the right direction isn't blind or unknowing. It actually is a pretty reasonable thing to do, considering that for more than two thousand years, millions of people have been led to places of deep joy and certain truth by those very maps.

So before we go through all your confusing, sticky questions about Jesus, we're going to take a chapter to talk about the main teachers we have with regard to Jesus: the Gospels. We're going to talk about what they are and why we should trust them to tell us the truth about Jesus.

> Most of us read the Gospels with sealed and unwondering eyes.
> — Dean Church, *Occasional Papers*

And if you're not willing to take that step, you might as well just toss the map out the window, turn the car around, and go right back to where you started. Or you could always decide that you know how to get to your destination just fine, without using a map at all.

But where would either of those choices leave you? Back where you started or lost, gazing into the eyes of some suspicious, toothless old guy manning a gas pump in the middle of nowhere, who seems to have plenty more questions for you than answers.

Is that really where you want to be?

How do we know it's true?

Let's start from the top on this one. The top, of course, being God.

I'm assuming if you're reading this book, you're not a rank atheist. I'm assuming you believe in God, you believe God reveals Himself through Scripture and Tradition, and you believe the ultimate, fullest revelation of God occurred in Jesus. You may not understand it fully (who does?), and you may have lots of questions about how it all works, but your basic faith is in the God who loved you enough to create you and redeem you from sin and death through Jesus.

So we'll start there — with God.

Or rather, let's look at how God started with us and what the Bible, including the Gospels, has to do with that relationship.

God, who exists outside of and before time, willed all of creation, including human beings, into existence.

Human beings, almost as quickly as they could stand up, look around, and see what was what, decided that there just could be better things than living in perfect intimacy with their Creator. They turned from Him, did the whole forbidden fruit thing, and found — surprise, surprise — that they'd been wrong. Surprise, surprise, there wasn't anything better. Without depending on God, it seems, life isn't what it's cracked up to be. We call that whole miserable state of existence, separated from God by the weight of our ancestors' choices against Him, original sin.

> Certain new theologians dispute original sin, which is the only part of Christian theology which can really be proved . . . they essentially deny human sin, which they can see in the street.
>
> — G.K. Chesterton, *Orthodoxy*

Some people have a problem with original sin. They say it's bad for our self-esteem. They say human beings are really nothing but darling little bundles of sweetness who, given the chance, would never dream of hurting a fly, much less each other.

That would be wonderful, if it were so, but it's just not. Humans aren't totally depraved and corrupt — Genesis makes it clear that we're created in God's image and we're good. But we do have this stubborn tendency to misuse the will He's given us and turn it to bad. Need evidence? Watch the evening news.

I've Always Wondered . . .

But God, being God, didn't give up on us, despite our stubbornness and ingratitude.

Throughout human history, He has continually reached out to His children (that includes you!), saving them, telling them about His deep love, and welcoming them back into His arms. We call God's breakthroughs into human life *revelation*.

God revealed Himself through the history of the Jewish people — through the Law, through priests, prophets and kings, through victory and terrible suffering. The Old Testament, or Hebrew Scriptures, is the record of that revelation.

As good writers such as Saint Paul like to say, "in the fullness of time," God took yet another step to reveal Himself to creation, the most radical step of all.

He became a part of it.

You know it. Jesus of Nazareth, right? Fully human and fully divine, God made flesh, Emmanuel, like us in every way except sin.

Not too surprisingly, those who witnessed Jesus' deeds and heard His wisdom couldn't keep what had happened to themselves. Because, of course, this was it — God had mysteriously and miraculously broken into human history, conquered the sin and death we human beings had brought into the world, and was making it all right again, restoring His creation to what it was before we botched it. It was, in a way, the most profound love story of all time, don't you think?

So those disciples, and then their disciples, spread this Good News. Eventually, they started writing about it, too, so even more people could hear about it, and just as importantly, it wouldn't die out once the last witnesses to Jesus had left the earth themselves.

That's why they call Jesus the Word of God, by the way — if revelation is God speaking to us, then Jesus is the most concrete form of that revelation — a living, breathing, healing, forgiving, loving Word.

Now, let's take just a tiny break from God and think about your life for a moment.

Pretend you love someone. Maybe you don't have to pretend, but we won't be nosy. You can keep all that to yourself, thanks. Way too much information.

Anyway, there's this person you love. When you're in that maddening, yet wonderful place called True Love, you know that one of your most urgent, persistent desires is to make sure that other person knows how you feel. Whether you're in a relationship, or you're trying to grow beyond a "Staring-At-The-Back-Of-Her-Head-In-Algebra" kind of friendship, it's a priority, and if your emotions and commitment to the other person are real, there's no way you want any lies to be a part of that relationship. You know you care, and you want the other person to know it, too.

Why in the world would God be any different? If He's taken the trouble to constantly reach out to human beings, telling them more and more about Himself and the peace that life with Him brings, doesn't it make sense that He would also make sure the record of all those loving, saving actions was reliable?

If God loves us enough to create us, forgive us, and redeem us from sin, doesn't that mean He just might also love us enough to make sure the written record of all this love, forgiveness, and redemption is trustworthy?

That's exactly the way it works, and believe it or not, we even have a name for that aspect of God's care for us. It's called *inspiration,* and here's what the Church says about it:

> In composing the sacred books, God chose men and while employed by Him they made use of their powers and abilities, so that with Him acting in them and through them, they, as true authors, consigned to writing everything and only those things which He wanted.
>
> Therefore, since everything asserted by the inspired authors or sacred writers must be held to be asserted by the Holy Spirit, it follows that the books of Scripture

must be acknowledged as teaching solidly, faithfully and without error that truth which God wanted put into sacred writings for the sake of salvation . . .

— *DEI VERBUM* (A DOCUMENT FROM VATICAN II) 11

So that's the first big reason the Scriptures are trustworthy sources for us: God loves us.

We can trust Him to tell us the truth about Himself. Ponder this for a while. How could we even take one step in faith, if we didn't begin with that?

But . . .

But that can't be the end of the story, can it? You're familiar with at least one Gospel, you've heard more, and you may have even taken a class on the New Testament, so you know matters aren't that simple. For all of our talk about the truth in the Gospels, you know good and well there are inconsistencies. For example, the details of Jesus' birth aren't absolutely identical in Matthew and Luke, nor are the details of the Resurrection. Other details differ too: What's called the "Sermon on the Mount" in Matthew is described as taking place "on a level place" (or a plain) in Luke.

Knowing all this and more, you're perfectly justified in coming back to the question that started this whole chapter. Sure, it's easy to say in theory that God inspired the Gospel writers and protected them from mistakes. But how can these apparent differences fit with the idea of inspiration?

If God wants us to know the truth, why didn't He inspire the Gospel writers to get their facts straight?

Because . . .

Believe it or not, that is not a bad question. It's not even unanswerable.

Think about it this way:

God works in our lives all the time. *How* He does this is fairly mysterious — how much of life is our doing and how much is His — but there's one thing we do know about God's part: He takes us from where we are.

When God moves our consciences, gives us peace, or strength, He doesn't do it by suddenly jumping into our lives and making us completely different people.

He doesn't comfort us by transporting us away from the situation that's causing us pain.

He doesn't help us become better people by making us into different people.

No, God starts from where we are, and works with us to form and mold us.

We even have a term for that whole process: We call it "grace building on nature."

Consider the saints. Every one of them is a saint not because God made them into different people, but because God built on their natural capabilities to help them grow in holiness.

Sure, Saul's life changed dramatically when he was knocked off that horse on the way to Damascus, and when he wrote in his letters about being a "new creature in Christ," he certainly knew what he was talking about from personal experience.

But that "newness" wasn't about the fundamentals of who he was. He was still the same brilliant, bullheaded, strong, truth-centered guy he'd been before his conversion. It's just that afterwards, all of those personal qualities were focused on a new central relationship and a new purpose: spreading the Good News about Jesus.

What does this have to do with the Gospels?
Plenty.

I've Always Wondered . . .

When we look at the Gospels as sources of God's truth, we have to remember that very same lesson:

God worked with the authors of the Gospels to reveal His truth *within* their own limitations, including:

◢ who the Gospel writers were and their culture.

◢ the way they thought and their intentions in writing.

◢ their sources.

Let's take a look at exactly what God had to work with.

Who wrote the Gospels?

The word *gospel* is rooted in an Old English translation of the Greek word, *evangelion*, which means simply "good news." It's because of that Greek word that we call the Gospel writers "evangelists."

So who where these evangelists, anyway?

Even though the Gospels have names attached to them, names you could probably reel off in your sleep, the question of exactly who the authors were isn't a simple one. Many scholars, using the evidence provided by the Gospels themselves as well as ancient traditions concerning their authorship, conclude the following:

Matthew was probably a Palestinian Christian of Jewish background, but probably not the Matthew who's named as one of Jesus' apostles.

Mark probably wrote his Gospel in Rome and was possibly an associate of Peter.

Luke was one of Paul's missionary companions, and wrote both the Gospel that bears his name and its sequel, the Acts of the Apostles.

John was probably written by either the apostle himself or a close associate of his.

Now, you're asking, why did these guys happen to be moved to write down stories about Jesus' life? And how did they do it?

The Purpose of a Gospel

One of the most important things you have to remember about a Gospel is that it's not a biography as you understand the term. It didn't come into existence in the same way, and it didn't serve exactly the same purpose.

When you think about a biography, you probably have a pretty good idea of what you're looking for: a book filled with facts about every possible aspect of a person's life, written with no other purpose than to tell you all you need to know about Marie Curie or Neil Armstrong for that research paper you really shouldn't have put off this long, but...

Well, surprise, surprise, a Gospel is not that kind of book, which is why we call them "Gospels," and not biographies, in the first place.

It's not that the evangelists weren't concerned with truth and facts. They certainly were, as Luke indicates at the very beginning of his Gospel.

> *Since many have undertaken to compile a narrative of the events that have been fulfilled among us, just as those who were eyewitnesses from the beginning and ministers of the word have handed them down to us, I too have decided, after investigating everything accurately anew, to write it down in an orderly sequence for you, most excellent Theophilus, so that you may realize the certainty of the teachings you have received.* (LUKE 1:1-4)

Of course the evangelists were trying to tell the truth. Why would they bother to put pen to paper (or quill to parchment or whatever) if they weren't?

But here's the twist in the story:

The evangelists had a purpose in telling these true stories, and that purpose was to pass on the bigger truth: that Jesus was the Messiah, God's Son come to save all people.

So they told the story through that particular prism.

That happens to be the way all ancient writers wrote history, by the way. Whether you read Herodotus, Pliny, Tacitus, or even Caesar's accounts of his own battles, you'll find that ancient writers believed there was no reason to relate history unless there was a moral purpose behind it. History was written in the ancient world to teach a lesson — not just to communicate the bare, naked facts of what happened, but also why it happened, and what it tells us about human existence and ideals.

In that sense, the evangelists were completely a part of their time, and as we said before, God worked with them within that particular culture. He helped them communicate the truth about Jesus, not changing them into twenty-first century historians, but letting them be exactly where they were, allowing that purpose to shape which of the many stories that were circulating about Jesus they would use.

He also worked with them as people who had different and varied sources. How the evangelists used their sources is a pretty interesting detective story, but here are the basic facts for you to chew on:

First, we can assume that, as was the case with all ancient cultures, the first stage in the Gospels' existence was oral — the apostles and others passing down what Jesus had said and done.

Now, don't get all huffy about this, and more importantly, don't let anyone tell you that because oral tradition comes first, the record must then automatically be condemned as unreliable. Don't think that the game "Gossip," in which you see how twisted a story becomes after being passed orally through every person in your class, has anything to do with the reality of oral tradition in ancient cultures. Our memories may be lousy, but, as cultural anthropologists tell us, oral tradition in societies that depend on it is surprisingly reliable.

It's not difficult to see why, if you can imagine yourself in some other place than the intellectually lazy twenty-first century, where we have so many aids — notebooks, pens, books, and even tape recorders. We really don't have to listen very carefully to what a teacher is telling us, because we can always check our notes, check someone else's notes, or go back to the textbook.

But imagine if you didn't have all those crutches. Imagine your teacher walked into history class today and announced there was going to be a Very Important Test the next day, it would be entirely based on what happened in class today, but no one would be allowed to take notes during the class period. You'd have to rely completely on your memory. No crutches allowed.

You'd listen a lot more carefully than usual, wouldn't you?

The truth is, that's the way people in ancient cultures listened. They didn't have notebooks and pens to carry around as they listened to Jesus. If they were going to remember what He was saying, they had to listen very intently, and they did. Moreover, because this was a highly oral culture, people who spoke and taught tended to do so using methods that made remembering easier. Think of all of the sayings of Jesus, and how so many of them share similar wording. The Beatitudes are a great example, the way Jesus frames each by saying: "Blessed are you who . . . " and " . . . you shall be . . ."

I've Always Wondered . . .

Finally, if you're still not convinced, consider that these oral traditions about which we're speaking were not the fruit of one-time hearings. The apostles walked with and listened to Jesus preach and teach for three years to various groups of people. That's a long time to be focused on learning from one teacher. It's a good bet what they passed on was accurate, wouldn't you say?

The next step was the writing down of various aspects of this oral tradition. It's pretty clear there was some kind of written record the evangelists used in compiling their accounts, because there's a surprising amount of shared material.

Let's recap the process:

⌐ The apostles and others orally passed down what they'd observed Jesus say and do over three years of ministry.

⌐ Written collections of these sayings and stories started appearing.

⌐ In various spots around the Ancient Near East, in response to the needs of various types of people wanting to know about Jesus, the evangelists carefully sifted through this material and wrote down the essence of Jesus' life and words that was important for people to know.

So there you have a lot of answers to your questions about these Gospels.

Why do only Matthew and Luke begin their Gospels with the birth of Jesus? Perhaps because they thought it was more important than John or Mark did, or they had access to materials the others didn't.

> Instead of complaining that God had hidden himself, you will give him thanks for having revealed so much of himself.
> — Blaise Pascal, *Pensees*

Why are there slight discrepancies in the same stories told by different evangelists? Again, because they had access to different sources, first of all, but secondly, because of the needs of the communities for which they wrote, they'd emphasize different elements of the same story. We think Matthew was writing for a primarily Jewish audience, so he tended to emphasize how Jesus fulfilled Old Testament prophecies, a matter that Mark, who was probably writing for Gentiles (non-Jews) wasn't too concerned about.

Inspiration, the Sequel

We've gotten the four Gospels written. We've seen how God's grace builds on nature, using unique and limited human beings to bring us the truthful Good News about Jesus.

But we're not quite finished yet. How did the Gospels get from there to here? How do we know that in that journey, they weren't corrupted, or bogus gospels substituted for the real ones?

Well, we're back to the beginning again. We're back to trusting the map, but it's not the mapmakers we're interested in this time, it's the folks down at the AAA who give them out or the gas station attendants we're wondering about. In other words, who decided that these maps we're calling the Gospels were trustworthy in the first place?

In a word, it's the Church.

The leaders of the early Church were very, very concerned that the Good News about Jesus be passed on accurately. They didn't go around saying, "You know, whatever you want to believe about Jesus is okay with us. Just as long as you're *sincere* about it, we're satisfied."

Not at all. These early Christian leaders knew Jesus wasn't whatever we want Him to be. He is who He is. They knew that when we start moving away from that commitment to telling like it is, especially in relationship to God, we can easily slip into making God into our own image and using what we say He said for our own agendas.

So very early on, Christian leaders started sifting the wheat from the chaff in terms of the Gospels. They didn't do this arbitrarily, either. They were completely tuned into the traditions that accompanied various Gospels, took care to trace their origins back through reliable sources with care, and eventually decided, with God's help, that the four Gospels that we have are those that offer the truth about Jesus.

We find lists of these four reliable Gospels as early as the first century, and if a hundred years seems like a long time to wait, consider this:

The manuscripts we have of the books of the New Testament are, as a group, closer to the date of their composition and the events they describe than any other similar manuscripts from the period.

The oldest snippet of a New Testament manuscript we have is a few verses from John that have been dated to the early first century. There are several dozen other scrolls containing big chunks or, in a few cases, almost the entire New Testament from that point through the fourth century.

By contrast, for Caesar's book on the *Gallic War* (which took place around 50 B.C.), we have nine manuscripts, the oldest of which dates from the mid-ninth century A.D. — nine centuries after it occurred.

Tacitus was an historian who wrote fourteen books of Roman history in the early second century. We have four and a half of them, and the earliest manuscript dates from seven hundred years later.

There are lots of other examples, but you get the point:

Compared with other ancient documents, the manuscripts of the New Testament are older and much closer to the events they describe. Historians don't sit around seriously questioning the reliability of those other works, so it makes sense to give the same kind of respect to the Gospels, if not more.

Back to the map

Let's see where that leaves us.

You can assume that when you purchase a map published by a reliable source such as AAA or Rand McNalley, the vast majority of information on that map will be accurate and will help you get to your destination.

Our destination is understanding Jesus. We've decided our primary map has to be the Gospels, and there are plenty of excellent reasons to trust this map as a reliable one.

Let's go ahead and see where it takes us!

I've Always Wondered . . .

Remember . . .

- We believe God loves us enough to pass on what He wants us to know accurately. That's called *inspiration*.

- When we look at the Gospels themselves, we see that the evangelists intended to write accurate accounts. The differences we find are due, for the most part, to the different purposes and audiences for which the evangelists were writing.

- Early Christian leaders took great care to sift out the authentic accounts of Jesus' life from those that were bogus. They did this by looking at the content of the Gospels and tracing the traditions about their composition, accepting only those that could be traced back to people who actually had known Jesus.

- The manuscripts we have of the Gospels are closer to their sources than almost any other ancient documents are to theirs.

- The Gospels are unique documents, but because of the care with which they were written, and the concern of the early Church for truth, we can trust that the Gospels are reliable sources for information about Jesus. To approach the Gospels as complete skeptics ignores evidence pointing to their credibility.

CHAPTER 2

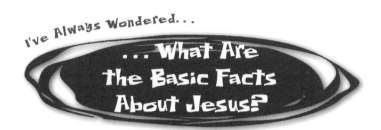

I've Always Wondered...

... What Are the Basic Facts About Jesus?

THIS HAS TO BE EASY. You're no professional theologian, but you do know this stuff, at least. Jesus was born, preached, died, rose from the dead, right?

Good start.

But you probably won't be surprised to find out that even basic facts about Jesus — which you have absolutely correct, by the way — aren't beyond discussion and controversy. You might already have discovered this, anyway, in an aggravating conversation or two with friends of various religious persuasions.

Your nonbelieving friend, for example, might have very coolly told you over your slab of cardboard, a.k.a. school cafeteria pizza, that lots of pagan gods were conceived or born without human fathers — oh, and some other pagan gods died and rose from the dead, too, by the way. By telling you all about this in an impressively knowledgeable way, he might have caused you to wonder (just a little) if these themes of wondrous beginnings and miraculous endings were just plastered over the rather ordinary life of Jesus to make Him seem like the gods of classical mythology.

Your Protestant friend, on the other hand, might have laughed out loud when you told him that sure, Mary remained "ever-virgin" her whole life (as we say in the Nicene Creed). You might have wanted to laugh right back — that is until he opened his Bible and pointed out a couple of passages that, sure enough, refer to Jesus' "brothers."

It seems as if, like everything else with Jesus, even the basic facts aren't immune to argument. Let's get you ready to talk about this stuff.

The questions begin with the date of Jesus' birth. Believe it or not, Jesus was probably born sometime in the years 6-4 B.C. Before Christ. No, your eyes are not deceiving you. Jesus Christ was born (B)efore (C)hrist.

You see, the Gospel of Luke tells us Jesus was born during Herod the Great's reign as king (put there as a puppet by the Romans, of course) over Palestine. The very interesting problem is that this Herod died in 4 B.C. So how could Jesus have been born before He was born?

The confusion arises from the fact that around the year 525, a monk named Dionysius Exiguus decided to draw up a precise calendar of Christian events, using the foundation of Rome as his starting point. His calculations were a little off, though — he put Jesus' birth about three years after Herod's death, which, as we now see, was a big mistake.

... What Are the Basic Facts About Jesus?

So there you go — Jesus probably lived from 4 B.C. to around A.D. 28. Don't let the uncertainty about time bother you. We may be obsessed with time, surrounding ourselves with clock, calendars, and planners, but ancient people simply didn't share that concern. They were pretty casual about time, to tell the truth. Calendars might have been kept by governments and in religious temples, to keep track of festivals, for example, but most ordinary people were more interested in the rising and setting of the sun and the passing of the seasons than specific dates. Most people had only the vaguest idea how old they were, and there are countless ancient figures, including Roman emperors, for whom we don't have specific dates of birth. That doesn't mean they didn't exist or weren't important people. It just means ancient peoples didn't have the capability to keep exact time.

So it's not surprising that we don't exactly have precise records of when Jesus — a wandering Jewish preacher in a backwater of the Roman Empire — was born. Actually, when you think about it, it's amazing that we know as much about Him as we do!

So here we have Jesus — born in Bethlehem, a town about five miles south of Jerusalem. Bethlehem may have been just a village, but it was quite important in Jewish tradition because it was the family home of King David, the greatest king of Israel, who had reigned in the tenth century B.C. and whose descendants would produce the Messiah — the God-sent savior of Israel.

Because we've touched on the whole time thing, you're probably wondering about Christmas. Was Jesus born on December 25?

Probably not. Now, one supposedly fun fact you're going to hear, from a variety of nonbelievers, Jehovah's Witnesses, and even some anti-Christmas fundamentalists, is that Christmas is no more than a Christian adaptation of the pagan feast celebrating the birth of the Roman sun god. To trump the competition, the theory goes, Christians took over the feast and made it their own. That, the various protesters will try to convince you, somehow renders Christmas an illegitimate celebration. The nonbelievers keep jumping right to the conclusion that Jesus, therefore, isn't divine. The fundamentalists make their own leaps, too, but to the rather different conclusion that since Christianity borrowed or was somehow influenced by paganism in this regard, it had, by this time, been corrupted from its original purity, and that means you, Mr. or Ms. Christmas-celebrating Catholic.

Now, that may be (and I said *may be*) an accurate account of part of the Church's motivation for selecting that particular date to celebrate Jesus' nativity. But if it was, so what? That doesn't cast any shadows on Jesus' divinity or the Church's faithfulness to Christ. They knew they didn't know the exact date (remember — they hardly knew the exact date for *anything*), but wanted to celebrate the Incarnation (Jesus as true God and true man) anyway. In choosing to do so at the same time as the Romans were celebrating the feast of their imaginary sun god, Christians weren't embracing paganism (as the fundamentalist might say) or creating a story just to compete with the pagans (as the nonbelievers would say). They were actually doing a pretty smart thing — tapping into a sense of celebration already in the culture during that time of year and turning it toward the truth.

Matthew and Luke give us plenty of details about Jesus' birth, although not the same details, which some people see as a negative, but is actually a positive, don't you think? Matthew wanted to emphasize Jesus' similarity to Moses and how He fulfilled various prophecies, so he took care to include the Holy Family's escape from Herod (sort of like Moses being saved from Pharaoh's wrath when he was a baby). Luke was really amazed by Jesus' compassion toward the poor, and you can tell as much, even from the way he relates the story of Jesus' birth: He selects the parts that bring out the fact that God came among us through Jesus for everyone, especially the poor. In Luke, it's the shepherds, the poor guys who were hardly ever ritually clean enough to enter into worship, who get the Good News first, direct from angels.

With all their different emphases, there's one element that both Matthew and Luke share: the fact that this Jesus, whose name means

"God saves," was born of a woman named Mary, who conceived her child not by natural means, but by the power of the Holy Spirit. We call this truth the Virginal Conception of Christ — not to be confused with the Immaculate Conception of Mary, of course. That latter truth, which we celebrate on December 8, celebrates the fact that God saved Mary from original sin when she was conceived, making her worthy to carry Jesus, God Himself, in her womb. You cannot imagine how many people have those two truths confused. But you don't. Not anymore, right?

Is the Virginal Conception of Christ unbelievable? Well, I guess it is, if you don't believe in God, or if you believe that God is somehow limited in what He can do by human expectations.

> God is the great iconoclast; the Incarnation leaves all previous ideas of the Messiah in ruins.
> — C.S. Lewis, *A Grief Observed*

It's funny, but God actually spent a lot of time preparing us for this amazing event, in which all of salvation history focused on, as G.K. Chesterton said, "a young Jewish girl at her prayers." The Old Testament is full of stories of God intervening in the natural order to help couples thought to be infertile have children. Remember how Abraham's wife, Sarah, laughed when she heard she was to conceive because she was so old? (And that's what her son was named: Isaac — "God laughed.") The same thing happened with the conceptions of Samson and Samuel and loads of other kids, including, of course, John the Baptist.

God, it seems, has a habit of working miracles with women and babies.

It all comes down to this: the Virginal Conception of Christ was taken for granted by Christians from the very beginning. Mary outlived Jesus, physically speaking, and had plenty of time to tell the stories of His birth, stories which then evidently were passed on to the Gospel writers. There's absolutely not a shred of evidence indicating that anyone in early Christianity thought anything different about Jesus'

origins. The idea wasn't, as some would say, simply swiped from pagan mythology in the quest to make people believe Jesus was God, nor was it created to cover up an embarrassing, scandalous beginning to Jesus' life. Some people will seriously argue that with you, but all you have to do is ask for evidence, and trust me, all you'll get in return are not-too-attractive, totally blank stares.

So — Jesus was born of the Virgin Mary, and raised by Mary and her husband, Joseph, in Nazareth, a village way up in the northern part of Palestine, in the region called Galilee. Like most boys of the time, Jesus trained in His father's trade, which happened to be carpentry (Mark 6:3). He would have spoken the common language of the area, Aramaic, which is somewhat similar to Hebrew. One of Jesus' most well-known ways of speaking to God the Father is in Aramaic — *Abba* — which is an affectionate, familiar way of saying "father," more like "Daddy" or "Papa" (Mark 14:36).

Now, what about the whole issue of siblings. Did Jesus have any?

Many of your Protestant friends will say He did, pointing to parts of the Gospels that mention "Jesus' brothers." It's not as easy as that, however.

Those who translated the Gospels into Greek long ago were working out of two other languages: Hebrew, the language of the Old Testament; and Aramaic, the common spoken language of Jesus' time.

Neither Hebrew nor Aramaic has any word that specifically means "cousin" or "nephew." The only word they had to refer to any kind of male relative was "brother."

When the writers of the New Testament books (which were, we think, originally written in Greek) were pulling all of their resources together to tell the story of Jesus, most of the stories they'd heard had come down to them in either Hebrew or Aramaic. All of the references to Jesus' "brothers" that His Aramaic-speaking apostles had made and passed down were very simply translated into Greek, without really bothering to pick apart whether those relations were cousins, uncles, or real blood brothers at all.

Another good point to make is that there is a very important moment in which you'd think any real brothers and sisters of Jesus

Maker of the sun,
He is made under the sun.
In the Father he remains,
From his mother he goes forth.
Creator of heaven and earth,
He was born on earth under heaven.
Unspeakably wise,
He is wisely speechless.
Filling the world,
He lies in a manger.
Ruler of the stars,
He nurses at his mother's bosom.
He is both great in the nature of God,
and small in the form of a servant.
— St. Augustine

would be mentioned: that moment on the cross, when Jesus gave Mary into the care of His apostle John.

The implication is clear that after His death, Mary would be alone, with no one to take care of her. If Jesus did have real blood brothers and sisters, why did He need John to care for His mother?

YOU WILL NOT BE SHOCKED to know that Jesus was Jewish, steeped in the Hebrew Scriptures (our Old Testament), faithful in worship, come, as He says Himself, to fulfill the Law, not replace it.

As you well know, throughout their history, Jewish people have been subjected to prejudice and worse, and it still continues today — I've heard more "Christian" kids than I care to say use demeaning stereotypes of Jews, including as a part of their slang. Besides being terribly wrong, of course, it's more than a little crazy, don't you think? Our savior, Jesus of Nazareth, was a Jew who had nothing but reverence for the truth of Judaism, and yet some who claim to follow that same Jesus are anti-Semitic? Go figure. More importantly, don't just stand there figuring — do something when you see it happening.

So when He was around thirty, Jesus left His parents' home and began a ministry of teaching. His home base was Capernaum, a city on the shores of the Sea of Galilee — really a big lake about thirteen miles long and eight miles across. He taught, He preached, He healed and worked other miracles, and over the course of time (probably about three years, maybe less), He began to draw not only crowds, but the attention of the religious authorities as well, and not in a good way, especially as He brought His ministry south, toward Jerusalem, the center of the Jewish faith.

In fact, they were so profoundly irritated by the teaching of this rabbi Jesus and threatened by His words, that these same religious authorities convinced the Romans, who held the power of punishment in Palestine at the time, that everyone would be better off if Jesus were executed. So He was, using the most demeaning method the Romans had at their disposal — crucifixion in public on a garbage dump outside Jerusalem.

And that, everyone thought, was the end of that.

But it wasn't, of course. It was only the beginning.

IF YOU'RE LIKE A LOT of young people I've known, there are a couple of aspects to this Jesus story that drive you absolutely batty. Actually, it's not what's said, but what's unsaid.

What did Jesus look like?

And . . .

What in the world was He doing up until His public ministry?

That last question has a lot of subheads, by the way. What was Jesus like as a child? What were His teen years like? Did Jesus ever fall in love? Did He ever have conflicts with Mary and Joseph? Did He like to have fun with His friends, or did He just sit around all day building stuff and studying the Scriptures?

(Oh yeah — about that studying stuff. If Jesus was fully God, would He have had to study and learn at all? But doesn't the Bible say that "Jesus advanced in wisdom and age and favor before God and man" (Luke 2:52)? How does all that fit together? I know, I know — but you'll just have to wait until Chapter 9 for that knotty discussion.)

In fact, some kids even get irritated at the Gospel writers for not including that kind of information.

"Didn't they know we'd be interested in that stuff?" they wonder.

The fact is, no. They didn't.

Remember what a Gospel is. It's not a modern biography, reflecting modern interests in the everyday details of a person's life. If it were a biography, that's exactly what we'd call it.

But we don't. We call it a *Gospel* — a written account of the Good News of God become human in Jesus of Nazareth. The evangelists were interested in conveying the information most pertinent to that cause, not just heaping on all kinds of detail that really didn't relate. Not that they didn't know more about Jesus than they wrote, mind you. Listen to what John says at the end of his Gospel:

> *There are also many other things that Jesus did, but if these were to be described individually, I do not think the whole world would contain the books that would be written.* (JOHN 21: 25)

So this is what it all comes down to: The evangelists were doing some very focused work as they listened to the stories about Jesus passed down by reliable sources. They were focused because, from a very practical standpoint, their physical resources were limited: They couldn't run down to the office supply store to pick up another ream of paper to accommodate all that they knew about Jesus. For that very practical reason, they had to make choices about what was most important to communicate.

But there was also a theological reason for the evangelists' selectivity.

Think about the times you've had to relate a story — perhaps you had to tell your parents about a rather unpleasant occurrence at school, one that you wished had never occurred, but did nonetheless, right in the middle of English class, right in front of the very surprised teacher who had no idea you felt so strongly about Geoffrey Chaucer, one way or the other.

How do you tell the story of what happened? Even if you're committed to an absolutely honest retelling, you know you wouldn't have the time to go over every little detail of the scene, nor would you be able to go into an extensive account of even your own admittedly murky motivation for saying what you said.

Just like the Gospel writers, you're limited. They didn't have a lot of papyrus to spare, and your Mom's face tells you don't have much time to waste in explaining this mess. The Gospel writers had a very specific purpose — to give the world the evidence that Jesus was the

Messiah, the Son of God; and your purpose, while much different, is very focused and precise — to tell the truth about your actions, with a minimum of fallout.

That's all just a very long way of saying this: The Gospel writers, as much as we might wish they were, simply weren't interested in what they saw as marginally important detail about Jesus' childhood and appearance. In other words, they didn't care. They cared about the essence of what Jesus was all about: the loving, forgiving, saving Presence of God among us who'd preached, healed, died, and risen.

So perhaps we should take it as a hint: If that's what they were interested in, that's what we should be up to exploring as well!

Remember . . .

- The Gospels are books written with the purpose of spreading the Good News that Jesus is Lord.

- The information we find in the Gospels was chosen with that purpose in mind. They weren't written to satisfy our modern curiosity. They were written to help us see two fundamental and related truths: that God had really and truly entered history in Jesus, and Jesus is Lord.

CHAPTER 3

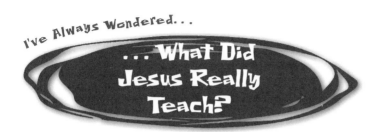

I've Always Wondered...

... What Did Jesus Really Teach?

I<small>T MIGHT BE A QUESTION</small> you don't think you even have to ask. You've been raised on it, heard the stories a million times, listened to readings, homilies, and teachers talk about it. You've heard it all so much, you could recite a lot of it in your sleep:

> *Blessed are the poor in spirit . . .*
>
> *Come, follow me . . . .*
>
> *The Kingdom of Heaven is like . . .*
>
> *There once was a man with two sons . . .*
>
> *I am the Way, the Truth, and the Life . . .*

And as you've been told from about year one, it's all about love.

God loves us, we're supposed to love each other. Treat others as you would like to be treated. Period. Now make a collage, color a worksheet or (worst of all!) answer these "reflection questions." Religion class 101 from kindergarten on up, right?

Of course love was at the center of Jesus' teaching. But as you've grown older and wiser, you've probably come up with questions that weren't really answered by your grade-school religion textbooks.

Aren't Jesus' teachings the same as those of other great religious and moral leaders?

What does Jesus mean by love, anyway? Is it more than just being nice?

There must be more to this. Never in my life have I heard of anyone being executed just for going around telling people to love.

In other words, you're wondering, what's so great about the Good News?

Love

Let's start with love.

> *"Teacher, which commandment in the law is the greatest?" He said to him, "You shall love the Lord, your God, with all your heart, with all your soul, and with all your mind. This is the greatest and the first commandment. The second is like it: You shall love your neighbor as yourself. The whole law and the prophets depend on these two commandments."* (MATTHEW 22:36-40)

Words to live by, of course. But just for Christians? Maybe you've heard rumors that the Golden Rule isn't exactly unique to Christianity. Those rumors are true. Take a look:

- *What is hateful to you, do not do to your neighbor: that is the whole Torah; all the rest of it is commentary; go and learn.* (Judaism. Talmud, Shabbat 31a)
- *Do your best to treat others as you would wish to be treated yourself, and you will find that this is the shortest way to benevolence.* (Confucianism)
- *... a state which is not pleasant or delightful to me must also be to [another] also; and a state that is not pleasing or delightful to me, how could I inflict that upon another?* (Buddhism)
- *Not one of you is a believer until he loves for his brother what he loves for himself.* (Islam)

What are you to make of this? Some people would like you to believe that the universality of the Golden Rule somehow diminishes Jesus.

I've Always Wondered . . .

See? (They say, chuckling.) *Jesus didn't really teach anything unique. You find something like the Golden Rule in every single religion on the planet. Therefore, don't you get it? There's nothing really special about Jesus — He was just another good teacher expressing some good, basic moral ideas.*

Listening to the debunker at the lunch table, you might be tempted to believe her.

Until, of course, you remember something important.

Jesus was executed as a lowlife and a criminal.

No one's executed for just announcing that it's good to live by the Golden Rule. It's obvious, too, that some part of the Golden Rule was *already* a part of Judaism. Why would Jewish listeners be so startled by Jesus' words and very presence if all He was doing was just running around Palestine telling them what they already knew about their own faith? Why would they drop everything and follow Him? There has to be more to the picture — more to Jesus' teaching, maybe even more to Jesus Himself.

> To relieve the poor; to clothe the naked; to visit the sick; to bury the dead; to help the afflicted; to console the sorrowing; to avoid worldly conduct; to prefer nothing to the love of Christ.
> — St. Benedict, *Rule*

(We can, however, learn something from the universality of the Golden Rule. Seeing as how the wisest people all around the world, throughout history, have figured out that it's a good guideline for life . . . maybe it is. You think?)

The Rest of the Story

> *Jesus came to Galilee proclaiming the gospel of God: "This is the time of fulfillment. The kingdom of God is at hand. Repent, and believe in the gospel."* (MARK 1:14-15)

It's a funny thing. Every one of the evangelists (remember — the guys who wrote the Gospels) begins his accounts of Jesus' public ministry recalling very similar words coming from the mouth of Jesus: He tells people the kingdom of God is near. He tells them to repent and believe. And He tells them, in a way that's clear, but still not what you'd call direct, that this loving, forgiving, and healing activity of God that we call the kingdom, has something to do with His presence. And by "His" I mean Jesus:

Just look back at what He says in Mark:

This *is the time of fulfillment.*

Or take a look at Luke, Chapter 4. Jesus reads a passage from Isaiah to a synagogue congregation, a passage that was understood to be about the Messiah, or the anointed one sent by God to save Israel. Jesus finishes, puts the scroll down and says,

Today, *this scripture passage is fulfilled in your hearing.*

A statement, you'll not be surprised to find, that didn't exactly thrill His listeners after they let it sink in. They were so disturbed, as a matter of fact, that they ran Jesus right of town and were ready to toss Him off a cliff.

Are you catching on yet?

We'll be saying a lot more about Jesus' teaching, but one of the things you have to get straight from the very beginning, something that we refuse to be coy or apologetic about, is this:

Jesus might not have walked around Palestine wearing a T-shirt that said, "I'm God." He didn't use the word "Trinity" or even spend time grabbing people by the collar and explaining His complete nature to them.

But the fact is, when you read and listen carefully, you see that every word Jesus said about those central themes of love, forgiveness, acceptance, and God's kingdom eventually points back to Him.

I've Always Wondered . . .

The Good News isn't just that God loves us.

It's that God loves us so much He became one of us.

The Good News isn't just that God forgives us.

It's that this forgiveness is offered to us through Jesus, in words we can understand because they're spoken in the language of human beings.

The Good News isn't just that God is present everywhere.

It's that God is present among us as a human being, telling us in plain language what life is all about.

The Good News isn't just about vague promises of immortality.

It's about the absolutely clear witness of a crucified man, raised from the dead, who promises the exact same joyful future to those who would dare to place their lives in this same man's hands.

In other words, the Good News is exactly what Jesus says it is:

> "This is the time of fulfillment. The kingdom of God is at hand."

It is the love of the eternal, immortal God made concrete on earth through Jesus, the carpenter's son from Galilee.

It's clear Jesus was no ordinary rabbi. His preaching and parables embodied a message that was bound to disturb almost as much as it comforted, depending on your point of view. It might even get you crucified, if you didn't watch out.

> I have read in Plato and Cicero sayings that are very wise and very beautiful; but I never read in either of them: "Come unto me all ye that labour and are heavy laden and I shall give thee rest."
>
> — St. Augustine

God

Jesus, of course, was Jewish, and the crowds He taught were mostly Jewish. He and His listeners shared a common spiritual background. To really get what Jesus says about God, then, you have to have a good grasp of what Jewish tradition said about God, and what aspects of that tradition were in need of clarification by Jesus' time.

Remember, for just a minute, that Jesus is the climax of that huge saga we call salvation history — the story of God's constant attempts to tell and show us who He is and why He created us in the first place.

A coach doesn't stop a practice when everything's going great. She interrupts a drill or an informal scrimmage when you guys are messing up, forgetting your technique and, in general, veering way off track.

That's what all these startling movements of God into human history are about, too. God's always present, of course, but there are times in which we forget Him and what He's really about, so He has to stop us in our tracks and point us in the right direction again.

Of course, Jesus' listeners already believed in God. They knew there's only one God, they knew He was their Creator, and that the fullest, deepest happiness in life is found in serving Him. No problem there. But, as Jesus makes clear, there were things that had been forgotten.

God's Love

There's a particularly lazy way of trying to understand this, but really, it's just a mindless caricature. What I'm talking about is the idea that:

The God of the Old Testament is the God of judgment.
The God of the New Testament is the God of love.

Okay. If you think that's true, take a look at these two Scripture passages and tell me which is from the Old Testament and which is from the New:

> *Thus it will be at the end of the age. The angels will go out and separate the wicked from the righteous and throw them into the fiery furnace, where there will be wailing and grinding of teeth.*

And:

> *Can a mother forget her infant,*
>   *be without tenderness for the child of her womb?*
> *Even should she forget,*
>   *I will never forget you.*
> *See, upon the palms of my hands I have written*
>   *your name . . .*

That's right. The words about the unrepentant suffering in hell? That was Jesus talking (Matthew 13:49-50). And the tender reminder about the strength of God's love? That's from Isaiah (49:15-16). In the Old Testament.

The truth is, God is beyond our complete understanding. If He weren't, He wouldn't be God, would He now? (To see how true this is, try to define who you are in one paragraph. Can you do it? I doubt it, and more importantly, I'd be worried if you could. So, if you can't define yourself with words, how can you get ticked off at God for being beyond the same kind of definition?) But even if God can't be totally comprehended by our limited human minds, He can be known, especially in the ways He reveals Himself to us.

So, as we've learned through God's revelation in the Old Testament, God is the Creator and sustainer of all that is. He is spirit, not flesh, yet we can be in a personal relationship with Him. He brought human beings into existence out of love, and He wants us to work with Him so creation reflects who He is: Love, Justice, Peace, Truth, and Life.

Obviously, Jesus' listeners, formed by the Law and the prophets, knew this. But just as clearly, some aspects of God were being neglected or forgotten. These are the points Jesus emphasized, not only through His words, but also through His actions, so that people not only heard them, but also saw these elements of God active and working right in front of them, through Jesus:

> *Our Father in heaven* (MATTHEW 6:9).

Jesus was very clear about this, wasn't He? God isn't a feeling inside you, an abstract Higher Power, or a bright, shiny Force. God created each of us on purpose, out of love, and He never stops loving us, either. He's a distinct spiritual being, mysteriously among us, as intimate to our being as a parent, yet transcendent and completely distinct from us.

> *Your kingdom come* (MATTHEW 6:10).

As you saw near the beginning of this chapter, this thing called the "kingdom of God" (or heaven) is all over Jesus' teachings. What is it exactly?

Simply put, the kingdom of God is God's presence. So you'll stop that annoying habit of thinking of the kingdom of God as a physical place, sometimes it's best to think of it as the "reign of God" instead. It's kind of mysterious — Jesus talks about the kingdom of God being near, but He also talks about it being among us (Luke 17:20-21). In

I've Always Wondered . . .

other words, it's "Already, but not yet." We are invited to submit our-selves to God's reign in our lives now, but because there's still sin in the world, that reign — that kingdom of God — won't come in its fulfill-ment until sin has been completely defeated.

Jesus tends to talks about the kingdom of God quite a bit, and with a rather specific emphasis: Through His words and actions both, Jesus makes clear that every single person is welcome into that kingdom.

You see, the problem was that many of His contemporaries, par-ticularly those who were members of a subgroup called the Pharisees, had come to believe that God's favor was limited to those who were able to observe the Jewish Law in all its great detail, covering every-thing from what you were allowed to eat to what activities you were allowed to perform on the Sabbath.

If you're even vaguely familiar with the Gospels, you've noticed this was a huge point of conflict between Jesus and many Jewish leaders.

Jesus regularly associated with people that would, according to the Law, render Him "unclean" — that is, unable to worship in the Tem-ple — people such as tax collectors, prostitutes, and all sorts of sin-ners. There were objections, of course. A bit of scandal. But what did Jesus say?

Those who are well do not need a physician, but the sick do.
(MATTHEW 9:12)

Jesus regularly broke Sabbath regulations: He healed on the Sab-bath, which would have been considered work, as was the simple action of walking through a field and picking grain to eat. Another scandal. But here's what Jesus has to say:

The sabbath was made for man, not man for the Sabbath.
(MARK 2:27)

Don't get the wrong idea, though. Jesus wasn't saying the Law was useless. In fact, He said the exact opposite:

Do not think that I have come to abolish the law or the prophets. I have come not to abolish but to fulfill.
(MATTHEW 5:17)

So what's going on here?

Look at it this way. The Law, as given to Moses and developed over time by the people of Israel, was part of God's revelation. It was the way God taught the Jews, and the rest of the world as well, how to live and what we, as God's children, should value: life, truth, compassion, and justice.

Over time, the understanding of the Law got a little off track. Some people began to think that God's attitude toward them was defined by their observance of the Law. So once again, God intervened — through Jesus this time — not to throw the Law out the window, but to re-reveal its true purpose, which was to help people see that God's gift of life is almost as holy as God Himself is, and should be treated as such.

Jesus' actions of loving, healing, forgiving, and teaching fulfilled the Law because He was trying to help people reach back to its original purpose and fundamental spirit. (Take a look at Matthew 5:21-48 to get a sense of this.)

Now, let's get back to the kingdom of God and see how this all works together.

Jesus is saying that the kingdom isn't defined by the Law — it's defined by God's presence, which isn't limited, and can't be.

Anyone, Jesus says, no matter whether they're a Gentile or a Jew, no matter whether or not the Law defines them as defiled, can be embraced by God's love and forgiveness.

So does this mean anything goes? Does God loving us as we are mean that everything about us is just fine with Him? Let's look at the next line of the Lord's Prayer to figure out the answer to that one.

Forgive us our sins. (LUKE 11:4)

This is a big one, and the most scandalous of all.

First, let's backtrack and look at what sin is and what it does to us.

You, I and every blessed sinner on the planet would like to think that God's love means God's total approval of everything we do and think we are, but it's just not so. If you find yourself resisting this idea, just shift your thinking away from your own behavior, which you'd simply love to see excused and accepted, and consider someone else's.

Have you ever been the victim of a bully? What kind of universe would this be if God's love of that bully (which is real, and powerful, and just as passionate as His love for you) meant that He loved the bully "just as he is" — including all his dreadful, hurtful behavior?

If that were the case, you have to think, this universe that God created would really be a terrible place with no morality and no justice. But that's not the way it is — God loves us passionately to the core of our being as He created us. Sin distorts that image. Sin puts other things in the place of God, and brings incredible wreckage to the creation that was once beautiful and strong.

Notice, if you can, that Jesus' presence among sinners never excuses their sins or allows them to go unnoticed. He tells the woman caught in adultery to "Go, and sin no more." Whenever the unwanted — such as lepers — or the scandalous — such as tax collectors — come to Jesus, we see two things: acceptance of the person as a loved child of God, and healing — either of illness or of the soul sickness caused by sin. Sinners don't come to Jesus expecting an acceptance of their sin. They come to Him, obviously, for forgiveness of their sin and the strength to go on after Jesus has gone to the next town, to continue to live in God's mercy, free from sin.

What Jesus was fighting against, both in the religion of His time and in the human heart, was the way sin works to keep us from God.

This is the way it usually goes in our lives: Think of any persistent sinful behavior you're burdened by. Let's take a really bad case: You've been looking at stuff on the Internet that you really, really know you shouldn't be anywhere near. Think of how this affects your relation-ship with God for a minute.

Though you don't mean it to, when you start getting involved in sinful activity or thoughts, your self-definition shifts, just a little. All of a sudden, there's a part of you that doesn't belong to God anymore, a part that you would keep secret from God, if only you could. There's a little area of your life that you've built a wall around, trying to keep God out.

At that moment, you have officially started the process of letting yourself be defined by your involvement in sin, rather than God's love for you.

Doesn't it feel good? No? Gee. I wonder why.

Well, since we're not feeling so wonderful about ourselves any-more, why don't we see what Jesus has to say to sinners — and that means us, of course: Our sins don't define us. We can be free of them, and once again allow God's love to define us. When we see that, we see ourselves in a whole other, better light and even find the grace to live that way.

Now turn off that computer and get rid of those files, okay?

Back to Jesus. As usual, He didn't just talk about this stuff. He did something about it, too, and that's what got Him into real trouble.

You may be surprised to find out that Jewish leaders weren't par-ticularly upset by the fact that Jesus healed illness. No, what really got them was that Jesus claimed the authority to forgive sins — not just of those who'd sinned against Him, but to offer some sort of cosmic pardon of wrongdoing.

Like He was God or something, you know?

> *He said to her, "Your sins are forgiven." The others at table*
> *said to themselves, "Who is this who even forgives sins?"*
> (Luke 7:48-49)

Who in the world does this guy think He is?

I've Always Wondered . . .

There's more of course: Jesus taught pretty consistently about the uselessness of material possessions and the folly of all of us who hoard stuff and are dumb enough to think that any of the things we've got stuffed in our closets, garages, or bank accounts are going to bring us happiness. Jesus taught that the path of holiness is really, really hard — it's a narrow gate, it might involve turning our back on all we hold dear, even our families, and it almost always involves a cross — maybe one made of wood, or maybe one made of people's scorn. It doesn't matter. It's still a cross, it still hurts — unless we let Him carry it for us, of course.

> We all long for heaven where God is, but we have it in our power to be in heaven with Him right now — to be happy with Him at this very moment. But being happy with Him now means loving like He loves, helping like He helps, giving as He gives, serving as He serves, rescuing as He rescues, being with Him twenty-four hours a day — touching Him in his distressing disguise.
> — Mother Teresa of Calcutta

So let's bring all of this together. Sure, Jesus is all about love, but now you see that when Jesus speaks of love, He's not just reminding you to be nice in a greeting-card kind of way.

The love that Jesus speaks of, acts out of, and actually *is* . . . it's passionate, strong, uncompromising stuff. It's a call to both accept and to give.

It's a call to accept God's love for you, and let that be the energy that drives you.

It's a call to turn around and give that same kind of love to every single person you meet. To forgive as you've been forgiven. To give life as you've been given life. To bind up all kinds of wounds, as your wounds have been bound by the tender hand of God.

And, finally, it's a call to see one more amazing miracle: God's love walking on the earth, sharing in our suffering, and giving us strength. It's Jesus, the one we call our Savior because He — and no one else — saves us from the deception that we're alone on the journey, and that love is a worthy, but impossible goal.

Remember ...

- The focus of Jesus' teaching was the kingdom, or reign of God.

- He articulated His message in preaching and parables.

- God had revealed Himself to the Jewish people through the Law, the prophets, and His intervention in their history. Through Jesus, God intervenes again, correcting their misunderstandings and expanding their experience of God.

- Jesus emphasized God's love and compassion for all people.

- Jesus indicated through His words and actions that this love of God was acting directly through Him. Where Jesus acted, the kingdom was present.

- We are a part of God's kingdom when we live in union with Jesus, strive to rid our lives of sin, and allow God to work through us to love others.

CHAPTER 4

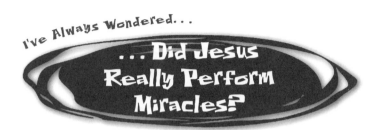

I've Always Wondered...

... Did Jesus Really Perform Miracles?

What's a miracle?

A DECENT GRADE ON A TEST you barely studied for? An amazing, come-from-behind, tail-end-of-the-fourth-quarter football victory? The fact that your parents didn't ground you for life after you broke curfew last Friday night? Recovery to health from the brink of death? Your existence?

You could — and perhaps you have — called events like these "miracles." But if you look at them closely, you'll find that you do so for different reasons:

- Sometimes we say that an event is a "miracle" when it's not at all what we expect should happen, or when it's outside the norm. Your parents not following their usual habit of grounding you for breaking curfew by five minutes would certainly fit this definition.

- Certain events seem to occur even though everything leading up to them would cause you to expect something different: Coming from way behind to win a game, beating an illness that kills most of its victims, or even passing a test you'd completely forgotten about — miracles all, with this definition.

- Finally, we often refer to something that is, at its source, utterly mysterious, as a "miracle" — the fact that a complicated creature such as yourself came from nothing more than the joining of two simple cells is a huge mystery, an amazing occurrence, and — here's that word again — a miracle.

There's nothing wrong with calling any of these events "miracles." Words can have lots of different shades of meaning. But let's avoid some confusion right away here: None of those meanings covers what Jesus did in His miracles. Turning water into wine, healing blind people and paralytics, raising a guy named Lazarus from the dead — these are in a completely different category from that last-second punt, right?

So here's where Jesus' miracles fall:

A miracle is:
A sign or wonder, such as a healing or the control of nature, which can only be attributed to divine power.
— *CATECHISM OF THE CATHOLIC CHURCH*, GLOSSARY

These miracles:
. . . attest that the Father has sent [Jesus]. They invite belief in him [Cf. *Jn* 5:36; 10:25, 38] . . . they are not intended to satisfy people's curiosity or desire for magic.
— *CATECHISM OF THE CATHOLIC CHURCH*, NO. 548

That's the official word from the *Catechism of the Catholic Church.* A couple of other definitions, which would cover Old Testament miracles too, might help:

An event whose only adequate explanation is the extraordinary and direct intervention of God.
— *Handbook of Christian Apologetics*, Peter Kreeft and Ronald K. Tacelli

A miracle is an unusual or extraordinary event that is in principle perceivable by others, that finds no reasonable explanation in ordinary human abilities or in other

known forces that operate in the world of time and space.
— *The Book of Miracles*, Kenneth Woodward

So it should be pretty clear by now: When we're talking about Jesus' miracles, we're talking about actions that . . .

. . . are extraordinary interventions into everyday life, and

. . .have a specific meaning that's related to faith.

But . . .

I knew it. I could see them coming, couldn't you? That big river of "but's" churning our way, coming at us, ready to wash away miracles in a matter of seconds. We'd better get busy:

But are miracles really possible?

That's a pretty basic question, and the best answer is nothing more than another question: Do you believe in God?

For you see, if you really believe in God — a God who's God, by the way, omnipotent, omniscient, omnipresent and so on — your answer is sitting right in front of you. If you believe in a God who is all-powerful and can do anything, well . . .

I guess that God can make miracles happen. Don't you think?

So there's your first step in figuring this whole miracle thing out: Think about God. Ponder God. Reflect on God: Creator of the universe, Creator of you, the Being who knows every blade of grass and every thought that churns in your busy mind.

It's hard to see, if you think about it honestly, how you can avoid the conclusion: Miracles? With an omnipotent God in charge? Well, sure. Why not?

> **For those who believe in God no explanation is needed; for those who do not believe in God no explanation is possible.**
> — John LaFarge, *The Manner is Ordinary*

Couldn't the Gospel writers have fabricated miracle stories to get people to believe in Jesus? Isn't mythology full of magical tales like that?

You're right, in a way. Miracles and magic seem to be pretty standard in mythologies and scriptures of every religion. But, as we said in a previous chapter, even a cursory reading and comparison of, say, Roman mythology and the Gospels shows a clear difference in tone and purpose: The Gospels are obviously rooted in real life, and while details may vary, both a commonsense reading and our faith in God's inspiration of Scripture should lead us to trust the evangelists as people committed to telling the truth.

We have to come back to that old point of motivation again, too. What motivation would the writers of the Gospels have for fabricating miracles stories? To convince people to believe Jesus was Lord for their own personal benefit? Why would they want to do that anyway? Were they going to make money off this belief? Were they going to win themselves amazingly high offices and honors in the Roman Empire? None of the above, of course.

In fact, those who spread this Good News — miracles, teachings, death, resurrection, and salvation — knew they were probably heading for fates that were the exact opposite: poverty, sacrifice, and perhaps even death.

So we have to be sensible. There was no motivation to make up miracle stories, and, as the writers themselves tell us in more ways than one, they were committed to telling the truth about a true story. They weren't interested in fairy tales. This was real stuff — the most important stuff in the world, as a matter of fact, because it was all about the One who'd conquered what seeks to capture us all: sin and death.

We can look at it from another, more complex angle as well. C.S. Lewis did this in his book called *Miracles*. He pointed out that in pagan mythologies, wondrous works always come out of the blue and change reality in surprising, and even shocking ways that really do seem inconsistent with the way in which we experience the world. A couple of examples might make this clearer:

The Koran is the sacred book of Islam, and one of the very interesting things about the Koran is that it contains stories about figures we find in the Bible, both Old and New Testaments. Even Jesus is revered as a prophet in Islam, and the story of His birth contains this scene:

> *And the throes (of childbirth) compelled her to betake herself to the trunk of a palm tree. She said: Oh, would that I had died before this, and had been a thing quite forgotten! Then (the child) called out to her from beneath her: Grieve not, surely your Lord has made a stream to flow beneath you; And shake towards you the trunk of the palm tree, it will drop on you fresh ripe dates.* (SURAH XIX:23-25. HOLY QUR'AN. TRANSLATED BY M.H. SHAKIR, MIHRAB PUBLISHERS)

It has a rather different tone, a couple levels beyond the simplicity of the Gospels, doesn't it?

Or take one of the miracles associated with Gautama Siddharta, better known as the Buddha:

> *Standing in the air at the height of a palm tree, flames engulfed the lower part of his body, and five hundred jets of water streamed from the upper part. Then flames leapt from the upper part of his body, and five hundreds jets of water streamed from the lower part. Then by his magic power, the Blessed one transformed himself into a bull with a quivering hump. Appearing in the east, the bull vanished and reappeared in the west. Vanishing in the west, it reappeared in the north. Vanishing in the north, it reappeared in the south. ... Several thousand kotis of beings, seeing this great miracle, became glad, joyful, and pleased.* (FROM MAHAVASTU)

I think we can see a huge difference between these kinds of miracles and the works Jesus is reported to have performed. As Lewis points out, Jesus doesn't do magic tricks. He doesn't do things that have no relationship to reality and the ordinary workings of God.

In other words, Jesus' miracles are, in a mysterious way, completely consistent with the workings of nature as God created it.

> . . . in all these miracles alike the incarnate God does suddenly and locally something that God has done or will do in general. Each miracle writes for us in small letters something that God has already written, or will write . . . They focus at a particular point either God's actual, or His future, operations on the universe.
>
> — C.S. Lewis, *Miracles*

When you look at the whole process, God turns water into wine through the normal processes of nature. God has given the gift of fertility to plants and animals alike, multiplying the wheat and corn that go to make bread, and making the waters teem with fish. All healings are ultimately rooted in the power God's given the body to fix itself. That healing may be prompted by medicine, or time, or your immune system. Or it may be short-circuited in a rather extraordinary way by Jesus' touch.

So yes, tales of wonders are everywhere. But the differences between what Jesus did and what other mythologies relate are twofold, and pretty convincing:

1. Jesus' miracles are related by reliable witnesses who had nothing to gain and a lot to lose by relating them.
2. Jesus' miracles aren't magic tricks. They're actions that are perfectly consistent with God's actions in nature.

But aren't there natural explanations for a lot of the miracles?

Ah yes, I've heard them all too. I've heard at least a couple of priests relate that what probably happened with the miracle of the loaves and the fishes was that Jesus' words moved the previously stingy crowds so much that they shared what they had hidden away. And Lazarus wasn't really dead. And the folks supposedly possessed by evil spirits were really epileptics. And that all the other so-called miracles were really just amazing coincidences. Somehow Jesus happened to be hanging out somewhere just as someone woke up from a coma or another fellow was able to blink the dust from his eyes.

Honestly. If you're like me, when you hear stuff like that you really have to wonder.

Why do people go to such lengths to try to disprove Jesus' miracles?

No, no, no. We're not against questioning, exploring, or analyzing. We're not advocating closed minds or thoughtlessly blind faith.

We're just wondering why, considering that whole motivation thing we just discussed, some people are determined to read the Gospels and fabricate all kinds of alternative explanations to events that are simply and straightforwardly presented as fact.

It's as if you were trying to tell a friend about what happened with your parents and curfew the other night (remember *that* miracle?), and he responded by telling you that sure, it may have *seemed* as if you were spared punishment, but you probably really weren't because that would be such highly unusual behavior, and just wasn't possible. You must have misunderstood. You must have been delusional. It was late, wasn't it? You were probably really, really tired . . .

So no, we're not going to even bother with any of those quite creative "alternative" explanations for miracles. To even begin to do so would be to presume that the Gospel writers and the witnesses who passed down the stories were, in a word, liars.

And if that was the case, why would we want to pay attention to another word they said about anything?

I've Always Wondered . . .

What Miracles Are and Aren't

It may surprise you that the word *miracle* as we understand it isn't an exact translation of any word in the New Testament. The events we describe as miracles in English are referred to as *signs* — especially in the Gospel of John — or as *works* or *wonders*. All of these words have something important in common: They all imply that these actions of Jesus are amazing, extraordinary, and have something to do with God.

Most people have a pretty standard explanation for Jesus' miracles. Maybe you've voiced this explanation yourself, maybe even on a religion test once or twice. It's this:

Jesus performed miracles to prove He was God.

Sorry. Wrong. You get an F-plus from me on that one.

Not that it's completely and totally wrong (which explains the F-*plus*, of course). All of those words are certainly related — Jesus — miracles — God. But they're just not related in the simplistic sense that phrase implies.

For you see, miracles weren't about Jesus' identity as a thing unconnected from His mission. If you need reinforcement on that point, just go back to the stories of Jesus' temptation in the desert (Matthew 4:1-11) and read how Jesus rejected Satan's invitation to do just that: to use signs and wonders to exalt Himself and attract attention in a very twenty-first century, publicity-seeking kind of way.

Nope, Jesus' miracles were about something deeper. Miracles, in Jesus' hands, were one more way of spreading the Good News about the kingdom of God, which is, if you remember, God's loving, healing, reconciling presence among us. Jesus talked about this kingdom. He told parables about it. He lived it as He welcomed the outcast and the rejected.

He did something else, too. He actually brought the power of the kingdom into people's lives, which He could do because of who He was: God Himself.

So Jesus' miracles were signs of God's presence that people could watch, see, and remember, saying, "Yes. This is what happens when we welcome God's presence through faith." (And don't forget what an important part faith plays in miracles. In fact, faith is integral to miracles. You might even say that miracles are a response to faith. Think of how many times when, after He's healed someone, Jesus sends them off saying, "Your faith has saved you.")

Miracles were works and wonders that actually brought the kingdom of God into the world broken by sin, illness, and death.

> The miracles of Jesus were the ordinary works of the Father, wrought small . . . that we might take them all in.
>
> — George McDonald

Just think about this: In Matthew 11, John the Baptist's followers come to Jesus with a question, one that they'd probably been muttering between themselves for a while:

> *"Are you the one who is to come, or should we look for another?"*

And what does Jesus say in response?

> *Go and tell John what you hear and see: the blind regain their sight, the lame walk, lepers are cleansed, the deaf hear, the dead are raised, and the poor have the good news proclaimed to them.* (MATTHEW 11:3-5)

So that's what miracles are about, and that's what they're for.

Jesus heals all kinds of illnesses because in the reign of God, all creation is restored to the wholeness that God intended, and sin is destroyed.

Jesus raises the dead to life because in the reign of God, death is conquered and life is eternal.

I've Always Wondered . . .

Jesus turns water into wine and multiplies bread and fish because in the reign of God, not a single person is in need: God provides, and we're satisfied with what He provides.

It's important to understand this point: Jesus' miracles aren't simply to "show that He was God" just so that people would believe. No, it all goes much deeper than that. It's not about Jesus showing, it's about Jesus being. It's not as much about proof as it is about the plain fact of the kingdom.

The Good News just keeps getting better, doesn't it?

Remember...

- A miracle is a sign or wonder, such as a healing or the control of nature, which can only be attributed to divine power.

- Jesus performed miracles of healing. His miracles also displayed control over nature (storms, wine, bread, and fish) and even death.

- Jesus performed miracles out of love for those suffering. The kingdom of God was present in Jesus' miracles.

- Jesus' miracles were all about faith: They were a response to faith, and they evoked faith.

CHAPTER 5

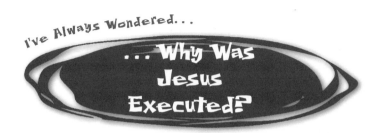

I've Always Wondered...
...Why Was Jesus Executed?

IF YOU'VE EVER BEEN IN TROUBLE, the following question will sound very, very familiar:

"*Why* did you do that?"

Why didn't you put out the trash, instead of leaving it as an invitation for a battalion of flies on the property for a whole other week until the garbage truck swings this way again?

Why did you pull the genius-like trick of writing the answers to that geography test on your arm, and then forgetting to roll down your sleeve when you handed in the test?

Why did you mouth off to your dad a mere two days after your last punishment for the same crime had lapsed?

Why, why, why?

In one sense, the questions are easy to answer: I forgot. I really needed to pass the test. I got angry.

But those answers only cover the superficial aspects of the crime, don't they? They don't get at the deeper questions:

Why were you so selfish?

Why did you embrace dishonesty as a means to an end?

Why did you disrespect and hurt your dad?

Why would anyone do any of these things?

As you can clearly see, cause and effect isn't always an easy thing to determine, especially when human beings are involved. Every incident — even the good ones — can be explained on a lot of levels. We can focus on the nuts-and-bolts reasons something happened: I cheated because I didn't want to fail. Or we can go down another level and explore the deeper reasons: I cheated because at that moment, I thought an act of dishonesty wouldn't harm my character, but even if it did, I didn't care, because I was so desperate.

> **The cross of Christ is the true ground and chief cause of Christian hope.**
> — Pope Leo I, *Sermons*

When we talk about Jesus' death on the cross, we run up against the same kind of challenge. We can (and we will) talk about the practical reasons Jesus was arrested and crucified: His words and actions threatened certain people who had the power to get Him killed.

As important and as interesting as those answers are, you know they don't cover the full implications of the question that heads this chapter. There's something deeper at work, and you know that because, as a Catholic, you're surrounded by images of this Jesus, frozen at the moment of His execution: crucifixes hanging from classroom walls. Stations of the Cross lining the walls of your parish church.

Why?

Why did Jesus die? What was the purpose of it? Why is it so important? Did it *have* to happen? Why does it have anything to do with my life?

Why?

Guilty as Charged?

As mystifying as the question of meaning is, even that first question of guilt can be kind of puzzling, too puzzling, given what you know about Jesus.

After all, when we consider the whole category of "criminal" — a category someone subjected to capital punishment certainly falls into — a person like Jesus doesn't immediately come to mind. He didn't steal, He didn't blackmail, He didn't kill. All He did was talk, and what's the crime in that?

In other cultures besides ours, plenty. You might be surprised to learn that freedom of expression, something you take for granted, is a relatively new development in human history. Until the truly revolutionary United States Constitution made something called "freedom of speech" a right for all citizens, most societies operated on the principle that speech was certainly something that had to be regulated and controlled, for speech motivated people to do things, perhaps even things that threatened social unity.

So, although things weren't as bad in the Roman Empire in the first century as they were in France in the aftermath of the French Revolution or in Communist countries, there were, indeed, boundaries of speech that really couldn't be crossed. Social, political, and religious unity were far more important than individual freedom to both the Romans and Jewish leaders during this era, so throwing someone in prison for what they said and what they refused to say (as was the case with the early Christian martyrs when they refused to deny their faith) was not exactly an unusual event.

But, you're wondering, how can a guy wandering around telling people to love each other be a threat? Isn't that what Jesus was all about?

Sort of. But if you read Chapter 3, you've learned that Jesus' words, actions, and very presence were, indeed, certainly about love, but not love in the quite superficial "be nice to people" kind of way we like to think about it. It was a love that challenged His listeners to welcome and live out God's love in all of its radical, sacrificial dimensions.

But to tell the truth, it wasn't what Jesus said about love that angered people. It was what He said about the source of those words: His relationship to the Father.

The Situation

Let's backtrack just a bit and sort out the players in this drama, which was no fictional creation, but history as real and vivid as anything that's ever happened.

These days, the land where Jesus walked is an independent country called Israel. Two thousand years ago, the area was still considered the Jewish homeland, given by God to Abraham and his descendants, but it wasn't called Israel, and it wasn't independent.

No, during the time of Jesus, the land was referred to, in general, as Palestine. Most of its inhabitants were Jews, but the country itself was part of the Roman Empire, and had been since around the year 63 B.C.

This foreign domination wasn't an unusual state of affairs — since about the year 587 B.C., with the exception of a century right before the Romans entered the scene, Palestine had been under the control of foreign powers, a situation, of course, that was a source of great pain: This didn't seem to be what God had promised Abraham, or what the prophets had foreseen as Israel's history. Over these hard centuries, the Jewish people saw hints of a better future, however. Those hints came to them through prophets and other sacred writings. They were hints of what they called a *messiah*.

In Hebrew, *messiah* means "anointed one." The Jewish people anointed priests, prophets, and kings as a sign of the role God had bestowed on them. The word translates into Greek as *christos* and English as *savior*. (Are you seeing the connection yet?)

The Jewish people had lots of hopes and dreams for this Messiah, but, in short, this is what they'd come to focus on by the first century A.D.:

- that the Messiah would be a king from the line of David (Israel's most successful and revered king who'd reigned from about 1004 to 965 B.C.).
- that the Messiah would restore the kingdom of Israel to its former glory and independence.

I've Always Wondered . . .

You have to understand that this messianic expectation didn't keep the entire Jewish population of Palestine up nights, waiting, but it was in the air most of the time, a situation that lots of "false messiahs" took advantage of before and after Jesus.

So Jesus taught and preached among the Jewish people of Palestine, people who'd been formed by an already twelve-hundred-year-old tradition of the Law and the prophets, and who seethed, quietly, but consistently, with the hope and expectation that God was soon going to free them from Roman oppression.

The Romans had many techniques to hold their vast, diverse empire together, and one of those techniques was to let the local people maintain most of their own culture (as long as they accepted certain aspects of Roman culture and honored the emperor) and have their own leaders — sort of. What the Romans did in Palestine was to collude with certain elements of the Jewish aristocracy that were willing (and no matter where you go, you'll always find oppressed willing to work with oppressors), and appoint leaders from among them.

The way it worked out in Palestine was like this:

The Roman official responsible for the area was called a *procurator*. His main responsibility was keeping the peace and collecting taxes. The procurator at the time of Jesus' passion and death was Pontius Pilate.

The Romans allowed the Jews to have their own kings and princes, as well. (This began as a way of keeping the peace after the Roman takeover of the land in 63 B.C. — they let the Jews keep the kings they already had). When Jesus was born, this king was Herod the Great. By the time Jesus grew to adulthood, Herod the Great had died, and the land had been divided among his sons. The son we're concerned with is Herod Antipas, who became the ruler (*tetrarch*) of Galilee, the area where Jesus grew up.

In addition to the political leaders, religious leaders played an important role in Jewish life. *Sadducees* were members of the priestly aristocracy who, in general, had little problem with Roman Rule.

Pharisees were teachers who interpreted the Law for the people, and interpreted it very strictly. By the way, before his conversion, Paul was actually a Pharisee (Acts of the Apostles 23:6-9). *Scribes* were those who copied and preserved the Law in each community. They were also teachers of the Law, (*rabbi* in Hebrew), and many of them were actually Pharisees, too.

A Tangled Web

There you have the lay of the land. Now let's see how it all played out, and why it ended with Jesus on a cross:

It's clear that from the beginning, Jesus made people nervous. He unsettled His listeners. His words even prompted them to violence sometimes.

Luke tells us that at the very beginning of His ministry, Jesus was run out of His hometown of Nazareth. Why? Because He read them a prophecy from Isaiah about the signs of the Messiah, and said, quite simply, "Today this scripture passage is fulfilled in your hearing." He then told them He wasn't surprised that they didn't believe Him, as the people of Israel had a long tradition of rejecting their prophets:

> *When the people in the synagogue heard this, they were all filled with fury. They rose up, drove him out of the town, and led him to the brow of the hill on which their town had been built, to hurl him down headlong.* (LUKE 4:28-29)

Do you get it? They were going to *kill Him*. And He'd barely even gotten started!

Something similar, although not quite so extreme, happened in another part of the country when Jesus drove a demon from an afflicted man into a herd of pigs (this was a pagan, that is, non-Jewish, area). What was the response?

> *. . . they began to beg him to leave their district.*
>
> (MARK 5:17)

I've Always Wondered . . .

So you can see that as popular as Jesus was, He was always walking on the edge. The most vivid expression of this, of course, occurred during what we remember today as Holy Week: On Palm Sunday, Jesus was welcomed into Jerusalem by crowds proclaiming Him the Messiah. A few days later, those same crowds called for the murderer Barabbas to be freed rather than Jesus, sending Him to Golgotha.

If all of that seems very strange to you, think again. Think about your own relationship to Jesus. Of course, you love Him and would never dream of shouting "Crucify Him!" along with those Jerusalem crowds, but the truth is that for many of us, our own reactions to Jesus are just as mixed up as those of the crowds. We're awed by Him. We know He's right in everything He says. We're moved by His love and want to be a part of it. But we're also scared. We're scared of the implications of Jesus' teachings for our lives. We're scared that if we really do follow Him, we'll be persecuted just like He was. We're like the crowds. We're like the apostles. We love Jesus, but way too often, when things get tough, we just run away.

Religious leaders were particularly puzzled, then increasingly angered by Jesus, for several reasons.

First, He criticized them, and no one likes that, especially when the critique is as harsh and pointed as Jesus' was. To get a taste of what He said, go the Gospel of Matthew and read Chapters 15 and 23. He points out, in no uncertain terms, how hypocritical they are, and how they miss the point of religious observance:

> *Woe to you, scribes and Pharisees, you hypocrites. You are like whitewashed tombs, which appear beautiful on the outside, but inside are full of dead men's bones and every kind of filth.* (MATTHEW 23:27)

This is actually a fairly complex statement: According to the Law, dead bodies were unclean — that is, contact with them rendered you unable to engage in worship, until you went through a purifying ritual. So Jesus is saying that while they look clean and worthy on the outside, spiritually, they're as impure as the most corrupt corpse. Plus, He's implying that they're spiritually dead, as well.

Strong words. Words that will definitely provoke a response.

Secondly, religious leaders were astonished and scandalized by the unique authority Jesus claimed. It was, in the end, quite clear that the authority Jesus rooted His words and actions in was no less than the authority of God Himself.

Jesus regularly broke the Law. He and His disciples picked grain on the Sabbath, and He healed on the Sabbath as well. In answer to their questions, Jesus very casually points out, not only that Sabbath observance should never be put before human need, but also that He, somehow, has more authority than even the Law:

> *For the Son of Man is Lord of the sabbath.* (MATTHEW 12:8)

Say *what?*

Jesus claimed the authority to forgive sins. The clearest example of how this brought Him into conflict with religious leaders is in Matthew 9:1-8. There Jesus heals a paralyzed man, but not before saying to him, "Courage, child, your sins are forgiven."

An odd statement, if you think about it. After all, I can forgive you for sins you commit against me (not that you'd ever need it, of course . . .), but can I look at you and say, "Hey. Your sins are forgiven."

Well, I could, but what would you think? You'd think, "What? She can't do that. How does she know what my sins are anyway? Why does she think she has the power to forgive all of my sins, even those that have nothing to do with her? Who does she think she is — *God?*"

Oh.

> *. . . some of the scribes said to themselves, "This man is blaspheming." Jesus knew what they were thinking, and said, "Why do you harbor evil thoughts? Which is easier, to say, 'Your sins are forgiven,' or to say, 'Rise and walk?' "*
>
> (MATTHEW 12:8)

I've Always Wondered . . .

You might note that we have two examples of these religious leaders witnessing a miracle — the healing of the man with the withered hand, and the healing of the paralytic. To our magically-minded brains, we'd think the miracles would be the most astounding, astonishing, scandalous elements of the story. But they're not. Not at all. In both instances, what gets the religious leaders going, what makes them agitated and even scared is that Jesus claimed God's authority — to decide what was right to do on the Sabbath, and to forgive sins.

The picture should be coming together now.

By the time Jesus went to Jerusalem for the last time, talk about Him and interest in Him had reached a fever pitch. A lot of people were wondering whether — and even claiming that — He was the Messiah, the one sent by God to free the people of Israel from foreign domination. It's not surprising that such a claim would get the Romans worried. Whether it was true or not, either way, the masses whom they sought to control and keep calm were going to be agitated.

The whole Messiah business was going to interest the religious leaders as well, but not in the positive way you might expect. First off, those among them who collaborated with the Romans were prone to share their fear of the agitation the Messiah thing was bound to produce.

Secondly, even the religious leaders who were anti-Roman and yearned for independence weren't terribly excited at the prospect of this Jesus fellow being the Messiah. Why? Because of all the quite interesting negative stuff He had said about them, of course. Not to mention this strange connection He constantly implied between Himself and God, hinting here and there that His authority was somehow superior to theirs because it was God's authority.

By the time Jesus got to Jerusalem, all of these threads were weaving together in a way that was bound to be harmful to Jesus, but it's clear He didn't care — in fact, if you read the Gospels, you'll see that Jesus' words about religious authority only got stronger as He got closer to Jerusalem.

So what happened? You know the course of events, so let's just summarize it this way:

One of Jesus' disciples, Judas by name, picked up on all the negativity about Jesus and decided he could personally benefit from it. He went to the chief priests at the temple and offered to hand Jesus over to them. They agreed, hoping somehow to stop Jesus that way.

Jesus was arrested and brought before the Sanhedrin (the Jewish council of leaders), whom He deeply scandalized:

> They all asked, "Are you then the Son of God?"
>
> He replied to them, "You say that I am." (LUKE 22:70)

You know what that's called, right? It's called blasphemy. To say that a human being, made of mortal flesh and blood, could actually be God's Son in a real, rather than adopted way (sometimes Israel's kings had been referred to as sons of God), was a grave insult to God, and therefore, blasphemous.

There wasn't much the Sanhedrin could do about the situation, though — they probably didn't have the power to execute all on their

own during this time of Roman political control. So they brought Jesus to Pilate (the procurator of Judea), who found nothing worth the punishment of execution in anything He said, and neither, according to Luke, did Herod, who was brought into the case because he was the ruler of Galilee, Jesus' home territory.

But, the Gospels tell us, the religious leaders kept up the pressure and so did the crowds gathered for the Passover feast — an occasion on which the Roman authorities would release any prisoner the population wanted. They repeatedly demanded that Jesus be crucified and that Barabbas be released instead of Him, and so Jesus was sent to die.

But why?

There you have it: A mesh of fear, envy, indifference, and even a bit of mob rule combined during those days to send Jesus, the preacher and teacher from Galilee, to a truly horrible death, nailed to a cross on top of a garbage dump outside the city walls.

So what?

Billions of people have died throughout human history. Some of those deaths are particularly memorable, too: Socrates being forced to commit suicide for corrupting the youth of Athens. Louis XVI of France and Marie Antoinette guillotined in front of the gleeful mobs of Paris. Abraham Lincoln gunned down in the balcony at Ford's Theater.

> It costs God nothing, so far as we know, to create nice things: but to convert rebellious wills cost him crucifixion.
>
> — C.S. Lewis

And each of those deaths had some impact, too — on their families, and even, in a roundabout way, on us, as they affected history.

But there's something quite different about Jesus' death, according to Christians. It's not just an event that teaches us a lesson. It's not

just an event that caused a chain of other events. It certainly is remembered for those reasons, but there's something else:

> *This cup is the new covenant in my blood, which will be shed for you.* (LUKE 22:20)

Jesus' death, so long ago, has something to do with people like us, living in the twenty-first century — it was actually, according to Jesus Himself, *for* us.

How can that be?

Can you imagine any other human being saying such a thing? When you think of your own death, can you even imagine your (we hope) 85-year-old self saying to your loving family gathered around, "I'm dying for you."

No, that just doesn't happen.

Wait — maybe it does.

A man stands on a street, looking in a shop window, thinking his small son is beside him. He looks down. The child isn't there — he's wandering out on the street, and within seconds, the horrified father sees a car bearing down on the very spot where his little son is standing. He rushes over, pushes his son out of the way, and places himself in the car's path.

He could die doing that, right? Why would he want to do it?

In 1944, in a Nazi prison camp called Auschwitz, a man was selected to die. He started to weep, mourning the lost possibility of ever seeing his wife and children again. Another man — a priest named Maximilian Kolbe — stepped forward and told the guards to take him instead. They did. Days later, Father — now Saint — Maximilian Kolbe was injected with a fatal dose of carbolic acid.

He died because of that. Why would he want to do it?

You could probably think of other examples — from the lives of the saints, from the lives of ordinary people who risked their lives donating organs or bone marrow, or who put their lives on the line in the process of rescuing someone else.

These are people who could say, "I'm giving my life for you."

It's called sacrifice, and it happens. People do it.

Jesus did it.

We're closer, but we're not completely there yet, are we? We've established that it is, indeed possible to sacrifice one's life for the sake of saving another's. But how does Jesus' sacrifice fit into that? He told His apostles He was giving His life for others, including them, but none of the apostles were about to be hit by cars. The billions of people who'd be included in the "many" to which Jesus refers aren't all standing with guns to their heads, waiting for Jesus to step in their places and take the bullet.

Not if you're talking physical existence, no. But, as you've probably figured out, that's not what we're talking about at all.

We're talking about spiritual life.

Let's do a quick refresher course in sin. Genesis tells us a lot of important truths, and one of them is about sin: Human beings wrecked God's good creation by sinning. Because of that, the world is broken, battered, and skewed. It's simply not the way it's supposed to be. If you've forgotten how that worked, go back and read the first three chapters of Genesis and absorb the truths it tells about temptation, sin, and consequences. It's no fairy tale. It's rock-bottom truth.

The rest of the Old Testament tells other truths, just as important as that first, incredibly depressing truth about sin. In story after story, it tells how God never gave up on His world. He constantly reached out — through patriarchs and prophets, men and women of faith, and events of disastrous proportions — to give human beings the chance to work with Him to knit the world back together. He gave the Law, with its grounding in reverence for life and justice. He sent prophets, who called Israel back to that truth over and over again.

They recognized the truth and power of God's saving love, too. They recognized that when they sinned, either as individuals or as a people, what had been torn — their relationship with God — had to be mended somehow. So for centuries, God's Chosen People engaged in rituals to make up for their sins to God: They offered sacrifice. Animals great and small, and even vegetation were offered to God as a way to reach back across the divide sin had caused.

These, however, were small steps. So, as the Scriptures like to put it, "in the fullness of time," God took the step of setting things right, once and for all. He came to earth Himself, taking flesh and blood, and subjecting Himself to all that is human, joining heaven to earth in the most astonishing way, a way named Jesus.

And sure enough, in a matter of just a few years, the world showed its true colors. Given the chance to listen and welcome God's reign, the world closed its eyes and blocked its ears and hung Jesus from a cross and killed Him.

I've Always Wondered . . .

But an amazing thing happened — just as God turned the Old Testament Joseph's suffering into good for the people of Egypt and Israel both, God turned this suffering into good as well.

Through this terrible death on a cross, somehow, in some way, the power of sin and death were conquered and laid low.

Blood shed for us.

One more sacrifice. The sacrifice to end all sacrifices. A sacrifice, not on a stone altar, but on a wooden cross. Blood shed, not so that our physical lives might be preserved, but so that our souls might be rescued. A Messiah would, indeed, bring a kingdom, but not one of this world.

Here's the point: Humanity's sin was a violation of justice. It was an offense against God's love, unending, passionate, and freely given. Whenever an injustice is done, it must be righted, or reality continues to be askew. You know this from home. If you've gone through a period in which you've done a bunch of stuff wrong — picked on your brother, neglected your chores — saying "I'm sorry" doesn't quite cut it. Even being sorry, as wonderful as that might be, doesn't put everything right.

> Cheap grace is the preaching of forgiveness without requiring repentance, baptism without church discipline, Communion without confession, absolution without personal confession. Cheap grace is grace without discipleship, grace without the cross, grace without Jesus Christ, living and incarnate.
>
> — Dietrich Bonhoeffer,
> *The Cost of Discipleship*

Something has to be done to make up for the wrong.

Who in the world can make up for the wrong that human beings have done and continue to do?

Can one of us do it? Certainly not.

Well, what if all of us, all together decided to make up for the sin that's wrecked our beautiful world? Probably wouldn't happen, right? And even if it did, you can see that all of that very human effort to somehow put things right wouldn't work and would fall short of what needed to be done.

Enter Jesus.

Enter Jesus, fully divine and fully human. When you think about, the only one who could bring this kind of salvation and redemption back into the world. He was human, so He was involved in the human condition, the human drama. He was a part of it in every way but personal sin, but because He was a part of it, He was subject to the effects of sin.

But He was also God, so through His sacrifice, the most stunning, overwhelming, ultimate sacrifice, sin and its effects — pain, discord, misery, and, of course, death — could be defeated.

That's why Jesus died.

But I think that fellow named Paul can say it much, much better than I can:

> *He indeed died for all, so that those who live might no longer live for themselves, but for him who for their sake died and was raised.* (2 CORINTHIANS 5:15)

No, we don't know exactly *how* redemption works. You try to figure it out, you fall right into mystery, and the more you try to explain it, the more meaning you strip from it.

Think, for a moment about love. A total mystery, right? Why does one person love another? Scientists try to tease your brain neurons and hormones apart to attempt to explain it. Psychologists delve into your childhood to try to do the same thing. But in the end, love remains. Powerful, transforming, and mysterious. It's there because we know it's there, and we live it every day.

Redemption is that same kind of mystery. We know it's happened because Jesus said it was going to at the Last Supper. He said His death was going to bring us forgiveness and eternal life. The apostles, inspired by the Holy Spirit, preached it to their own deaths.

We also know it because of the witness of Christians through history, what has happened in their lives when they have truly accepted that mystery and opened their hearts to the reality of Christ's suffering, death, and Resurrection. They experience just what he said they would: the forgiveness of their sins, the grace to live in union with Him in love, rather than trapped in the despairing snares of this world.

> The message of the cross is foolishness to those who are perishing, but to us who are being saved it is the power of God.
> — *1 Corinthians 1:18*

But explaining it, drawing charts and dreaming up all kinds of formulas for it, just doesn't work, because it's mystery.

And if you think that makes it unreal, consider love.

Powerful and impossible to explain.

But unreal?

Hardly.

Remember ...

- Jesus was executed for blasphemy.
- Jewish and Roman leaders also feared Jesus' effect on the people of Palestine.
- Jesus was executed at the urging of some Jewish leaders but by the hands of the Roman rulers.
- Through Jesus' death, our sins are forgiven and the world is reconciled to God.

I've Always Wondered ...

CHAPTER 6

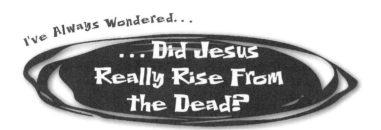

I've Always Wondered...

... Did Jesus Really Rise From the Dead?

SOME PEOPLE WORK INCREDIBLY HARD to think of something — anything — to explain away the Resurrection of Jesus.

The alternatives they come up with are fascinating. Just fascinating.

The apostles experienced a mass hallucination. Massive would be the word for it, too, if that were the case. Paul writes that on one occasion, hundreds of people saw the Risen Jesus (1 Corinthians 15:3-8). That's some hallucination, isn't it?

The apostles stole the body and hid it. Yes. Unarmed fishermen and peasants overcame the power and weapons of Roman guards. They rolled aside a huge stone from an above-ground tomb and made off with the body. That could happen. Sure.

Jesus didn't die on the cross at all. He sort of fainted and revived later, and the apostles made up the whole Resurrection thing to hide their embarrassment. Or something. It's proposed in a very popular book from the 1970s called *The Passover Plot.* I'm sure you don't need to read it to catch the problems right away. Jesus survived days of beating, torture, crucifixion, a sword stuck in His side, and then suffocating in tightly wrapped burial linens? Again — that could happen. I can see it. Really I can.

It's all a myth-take. The whole Resurrection thing — as well as the miracles — is really just a mythological layer that grew over the much simpler true stories of Jesus, stories in which the real Jesus roamed around telling people to love each other and accept God's love. This is a pretty popular way of trying to sweep the Resurrection (and Jesus' divinity, period, of course) under the rug today. But, although it sounds reasonable, when you look at the evidence, it falls apart really quickly.

We know that most of the New Testament was composed between the years 55 and 80 A.D., beginning about thirty years after Jesus' death. Thirty years is an awfully short time for such a detailed mythology to grow up. Besides, as we've pointed out before, the Gospels just don't read like any kind of mythology at all — they're too full of realistic, local detail, and too full of events that would tend to decrease their credibility in the myth-making world: women giving testimony, apostles denying their leader, and so on.

There's another big problem with these last two explanations. If Jesus either just fainted on the cross or the whole Passion/Resurrection thing is nothing but pious myth, there's one big question that's left unanswered here in the dust:

Where did Jesus go?

Either way, you're saying Jesus continued to live a natural physical, unresurrected life rather than what the Gospels tell us happened. If that's the case, what in the world happened to Him? How could this guy, a very popular preacher in Palestine for about three years, a controversial figure among Romans and Jews alike, just slip away and live anonymously?

And, finally, why would the apostles lie about it? If Jesus had, indeed, just fainted up there on the cross and revived, you can think of a million different responses the apostles might have had to that event, the most likely being that some might keep hanging around Jesus — who obviously would need some assistance, considering what He'd been through — but most would go back to their ordinary lives, perhaps better, wiser, and more moral men for the experience of having known this great teacher.

But leave home and preach a lie for the rest of their lives? Not likely.

I've Always Wondered . . .

The Resurrection happened in the apostles' hearts. Some theologians have concluded their deep studies of the New Testament, books full of material presented as the testimony of eyewitnesses, crammed with detail and rooted in the experience of Jesus really and truly risen from the dead, by saying that what *really* happened wasn't a resurrection at all, as we normally think of it. What happened, they say, is that somehow, after Jesus' crucifixion, the apostles finally came to a full understanding of Jesus' teaching. Through an interior mystical experience, they came to see that Jesus was, indeed, intimately related to God, that He'd mediated God's love during His time on earth, and that He was with God now, experiencing eternal life.

So sure, Jesus lived — with God and in the apostles' hearts and ministry. But Resurrected, body and soul? Nah. And the stories? Well, explanations vary, but it seems what basically happened is that the apostles' experience of the living Jesus was so real, the only way they could describe it was to write it as if it were the physical Jesus in their midst, like a metaphor.

Beyond these last three explanations are a few more interesting suggestions:

There's one very famous New Testament scholar, retired from the faculty of a Catholic university, who has a fascinating explanation of the Resurrection. He doesn't deny that the apostles found an empty tomb. He just says that the reason the tomb was empty was because a pack of wild dogs had stolen Jesus' body.

Really.

Another theory, again one proposed by another scholar, is that in that post-crucifixion haze, the apostles went to a tomb, and it was an empty tomb, but it was empty for a reason: It was the wrong tomb!

Whoops.

You know, the Gospels writers never hesitate to present the apostles as the flawed human beings they were, and one of their faults, regularly pointed out by Jesus Himself, was, to put it delicately, a rather frequent failure of perception. But I'm sure you're with me in failing to see how they could be *that* dumb — to show up at the wrong tomb, not look for the right one once they found it strangely empty, and then start a whole religious movement based on that.

We need to cut to the chase here. Almost every one of these alternative theories (except for the hallucination one) rests on a single premise:

The apostles lied. For some reason — they were humiliated by the death of Jesus, didn't know what to do with the fact that He never died in the first place, or they were just dumb — the whole Resurrection scenario as presented in the Gospels, including Jesus appearing, Jesus giving the Holy Spirit to the apostles, Jesus letting Thomas touch His wounds, Jesus ascending, the whole thing was fabricated.

As we've pointed out before, logically speaking, that just doesn't work. Sure, lots of people through history have experienced misunderstandings and misperceptions of reality. They've seen things that weren't there and told lies.

But consider this: Is it consistent with anything you've ever heard about or seen in your life to suggest that the apostles lied about Jesus' Resurrection?

For any of these theories to be true, a lot would have had to accompany it:

All of the apostles — every single one — would have had to go through the rest of their lives holding up this lie as truth. They would have had to maintain the deceit under the threat of persecution and torture.

All of the apostles would have abandoned their homes and previous lives to spread out through the entire Mediterranean area (and India, in the case of Thomas) and devote the rest of their lives to telling others about the lie and getting them to buy into it.

All of the apostles would have done this without any financial or social gain, and in fact, would have been doing it at a considerable price.

The lie — whichever one it happened to be — would be continually presented as truth in the relatively small geographical area called Judea, without being exposed by any of the scores of people who undoubtedly would have known the real story.

That, as many people have pointed out, would have been almost more of a miracle than the Resurrection itself!

No, when you look at the evidence objectively and consider the realities of human life, you really can't escape the logical conclusion:

This really happened. Jesus of Nazareth, who died a very public death and was buried in a heavily guarded tomb, rose from the dead.

It's true. He's alive.

Now what does it mean?

"God Raised Him Up"

These days, if you're not careful, you might just come to believe that the heart of Christianity was no more than the Golden Rule. After all, that's how it's presented, even by religion teachers, more often than not.

But that's just not true. As we've said over and over, radical *agape* love is central, but it's not the core. If you want to know what that core is, all you need to do is go to the New Testament and see what the apostles, the guys who were there and really should know, said about it. What was the central theme of their preaching?

> We ourselves are proclaiming this good news to you that what God promised our ancestors he has brought to fulfillment for us, [their] children, by raising up Jesus . . .
> (ACTS 13:32-33)

Paul, the one who spoke those words, wrote about the importance of the Resurrection in his first letter to the Corinthians, also:

> And if Christ has not been raised, then empty [too] is our preaching; empty, too, your faith . . . if Christ has not been raised, your faith is vain; you are still in your sins.
> (1 CORINTHIANS 15:14,17)

What this early preaching, so close to the time of Jesus, tells us is that without the Resurrection, there's no Christianity. Without the Resurrection, reality remains just as it was before: Sin keeps its power over us, and death is really the end.

In other words, contrary to what you may have heard, the Resurrection of Jesus doesn't just "show" us something. It's not there to just inspire us to suffer for the cause of right, knowing that good eventually wins.

No — the Resurrection changes reality. Through Jesus' death and Resurrection, life as we know it is transformed into life as we always knew it should be.

One way to see it is like this: Sin killed Jesus. Not just the sin of the crowds or the religious and political leaders, but the whole web of sin brought into the world by our first parents and readily embraced by us. Sin — their sin and our sin, too — killed Jesus. As happens every day, human beings, deep in sin, turned from God and turned on God,

I've Always Wondered . . .

Make no mistake: if He rose at all
It was as His body;
If the cells' dissolution did not reverse, the
 molecules reknit, the amino acids rekindle,
The Church will fall.

Let us not mock God with metaphor,
Analogy, sidestepping transcendence;
Making of the event a parable, a sign painted
 in the faded credulity of earlier ages:
Let us walk through the door.
— John Updike, *Easter*

seeking to nail Him into silence so they could go on their (our) not-so-merry destructive ways.

Sin wins these battles a lot. It not only wins, it spreads the spoils of victory wherever it may and brings lots of destruction in its wake. To know this is true, read the first eleven chapters of Genesis and see how one choice eventually leads to the corruption of the entire world. To know this is true, think about your own sins — your laziness, your disrespect, your dishonesty — and consider how those habits, thoughts, tendencies, and actions slowly but surely bend your character, and how all of that eventually introduces more discord and evil into other people's lives.

Back to Jesus. As we said, sin has a lot of power — it even has the power to kill us, body and soul. On a Friday afternoon in Jerusalem, Jesus was at the receiving end of this power.

For a few days, it looked as though Jesus' confrontation with sin and death had ended the same way it does for all of us: with a closed door, sadness, and rotting flesh.

But, it turns out, this time was different.

> What reason have atheists for saying that we
> cannot rise again? Which is the more difficult, to
> be born, or to rise again? That what has never
> been, should be, or that what has been, should be
> again? Is it more difficult to come into being
> than to return to it?
>
> — Pascal, *Pensees*

This time, sin lost. Death lost, too — it was totally, absolutely defeated by God's power.

Jesus rose. The sin couldn't corrupt Him. Death couldn't kill Him. He was alive. Something was, indeed, more powerful than sin, more powerful than death.

Reality had shifted in an amazing way. God's original plan, disrupted by original sin, had been restored.

Do you see why the apostles were so excited now?

So What That Means for Us

As the apostles preached and the Church has taught ever since, Jesus' Resurrection is good news — *the* Good News — not only for Him, but for us:

> *We were indeed buried with him through baptism into death, so that, just as Christ was raised from the dead by the glory of the Father, we too might live in newness of life.* (ROMANS 6:4)

. . . and for all creation as well:

> *For in him all the fullness was pleased to dwell,*
> *and through him to reconcile all things for him,*
> *making peace by the blood of his cross . . .*
> (COLOSSIANS 1:19-20)

I've Always Wondered . . .

So what's going to happen, you're wondering. You accept the invitation of the apostles, the guys who knew Jesus, who witnessed His glory after the Resurrection, and who talked about this Good News they'd seen themselves for the rest of their lives?

You've probably already been baptized, so that means the grace of new life with Christ is already a part of your life. You just need to embrace that gift of grace and work with it to draw closer to God.

Jesus was victorious over sin. That means, because you're joined to Him and to the grace of new life, sin doesn't have to be victorious over you, either. It means that with Jesus' life within you, you have the power to be holy — to be the fabulous creation God made you to be, instead of the easily manipulated slave to material things and your lowest animal desires that sin would much prefer you to be.

Keep walking with Jesus, keep dying to that old self, and you know what? Your physical life will not, cannot, and just won't be the end of you. Jesus' gift of eternal life is yours.

And remember — that's eternal life of your whole self, body and soul. It's important to remember that Christianity is a very holistic religion. We're not into saying that the body is bad and the soul is good, and that the body is just a temporary prison for the soul. Not at all — Jesus' Resurrection shows us what God thinks of the body.

For what happened to Jesus, the Gospels and Paul indicate, wasn't just the resuscitation of a corpse — that's what happened to Lazarus (John 11), but not Jesus. We know that because Jesus' post-Resurrection body was different than it had been: He could walk through walls, and wasn't otherwise limited by time and space. He wasn't always immediately recognizable, either, even by those who'd known Him for years. Something — we don't know what, and it was obviously too mysterious to even begin to describe in words — had changed.

Jesus didn't become a ghost after the Resurrection, either. He definitely had a body — He ate, He still bore the wounds of the crucifixion, and, as the experience of Thomas shows, those wounds could be touched.

So that's the Risen Jesus: alive again, body and soul, still Himself, but different in the sense that all the limits of mortality had been broken.

And that's what's in store for us: eternal life in which sin and death have been conquered, and our precious, unique selves created by God live forever — whole, restored, forgiven, and reconciled. At peace. In joy. With God.

It's all of a piece, really. Every bit of Jesus' life is about going back to Eden. It's about God, once again, walking in our midst, just as He did in the Garden. Jesus' words tell us about the love and peace possible when we embrace God's presence. His miracles make it happen in the lives of individuals. His death and Resurrection break open the world so everyone can not only see, but everyone can be a part of the restoration and reconciliation, too

If, of course, we have faith.

Do we?

I've Always Wondered . . .

Remember . . .

- All the Gospel writers report that Jesus rose from the dead. Beginning with the apostles, who were witnesses, the Resurrection has been a central truth of Christianity for two thousand years.

- All alternative explanations to the Resurrection rest on the assumption that the apostles lied and then based the rest of their lives, including missionary work far from home and even martyrdom, on a deliberate lie.

- Jesus' Resurrection transformed reality. The power of sin and death was broken.

- When we join our lives to Jesus and let His spirit live in us, sin and death have no more power over us, either.

 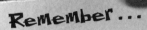

CHAPTER 7

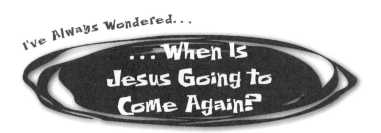

I've Always Wondered...

... When Is Jesus Going to Come Again?

WE DON'T KNOW.

Gee, that was a short chapter.

You think I'm kidding, but I'm not. Sure, there are a few things about the end of the world that have been revealed by God through Scripture, but not nearly as many as some Christians would have you believe.

You may have noticed that there are a few Christian denominations that are absolutely fixated on the end of the world and the Second Coming of Christ. People who are into this go to great lengths to explain their theories. They make big charts and detailed timelines. They point to newspaper headlines about this earthquake or that epidemic disease, and tell you these are the disasters Jesus said would directly precede the end of the world.

But do you know what?

> *You also must be prepared, for at an hour you do not expect, the Son of Man will come.* (LUKE 12:40)

Well, that was a big waste of time, wasn't it?

If you really want to understand the whole issue of the Second Coming of Christ, the first thing you have to do is ignore about ninety-nine percent of what you hear about it. Most of the talk you encounter is from the evangelical end of Christianity, and most of the details in their ideas about the Second Coming are, naturally enough, from that perspective, and rooted in a particular way of interpreting the Bible that Catholics — and most Christians through history — just don't share.

So if what I say in this chapter doesn't satisfy you, and you want to know more, head toward books by Catholic writers on the subject. Read what the *Catechism of the Catholic Church* has to say (which isn't a whole lot), study the notes in a Catholic translation of the Bible, and get some material from a Catholic bookstore. But don't — I repeat, don't — get caught up in popular speculation, because it is just speculation and as such, a huge waste of time better spent clipping your toenails, because, you know, they really need it.

Here's what we know from Scripture. It's simple, short and sweet — a welcome change from previous topics, let me tell you.

- Jesus is coming to earth again. How do we know this? He said so, repeatedly (Luke 21:27-28).
- He's coming for the Last Judgment of all human beings. He told us that, too.

⌐ At the Last Judgment, life on earth as we know it will end, and "the kingdom of God will come in its fullness" (*CCC* No. 1042). That means that the original order of creation, not just for the earth, but for the whole universe, will be restored and renewed. God's plan will be perfectly realized, and at last, just as He did in the Garden, God will dwell among us. We call this wonderful, spectacular restoration the "new heavens and a new earth" (2 Peter 3:13).

⌐ This final judgment and restoration will be preceded by turmoil, trouble, disaster, and even a few false messiahs and prophets.

And to tell the truth, that's really it.

Not that folks won't try to fill in the blanks and connect the dots. But that's all, as I said, speculation, and to tell the truth, it's kind of arrogant, don't you think?

One of the sources you'll find used quite a bit in these discussions is the Book of Revelation. It's important that you understand why using this book to draw up a detailed plot for the end of the world is just dead wrong.

First, that's not why it was written.

The Book of Revelation was written in the very last part of the first century by someone named John (maybe the same author of the Gospel of John, maybe not). It was written in the *apocalyptic* style, a style you find in certain parts of the Old Testament books of Daniel and Ezekiel. *Apocalyptic* comes from a Greek word that means "unveiling," and it's a style of writing that tries to tell the truth in richly symbolic language — if you even read a couple of chapters of Revelation, you'll see what I mean.

In the case of Revelation, we're pretty sure that this dense symbolic language was used as a kind of code. By the end of the first century, the Roman Empire had begun persecuting Christians, and, understandably, these same Christians were in danger of losing their faith and their hope in Jesus' promises because of it.

The Book of Revelation was written to restore and sustain that hope. It describes battles between good and evil, forces rising and coming to power, various afflictions and plagues sent to sinners, and, of course, the final victory of God and His faithful over evil. The symbols are really a code — the various evil figures, for example, stand for the Roman Empire and figures associated with it, written up in this way to disguise their identity to any non-Christian who might find the material, and thereby protect Christians from even more persecution.

Not that we can't gain hope from it as well. The language may be symbolic, but there's a whole lot of truth in Revelation, truth that's very useful to anyone who's ever wondered when God is finally going to get busy and handle the seemingly unending stream of evil that afflicts our world.

But a lot of folks read Revelation differently. They see it as a detailed plan for the end of the world, and they're constantly looking at contemporary events to see how they match up with what's described in Revelation. It's silly, it's a misuse of the text, and it's really an insult to the original intent of the author and, we can presume, God working through that author.

So hope is really the name of the game here. We know that Jesus is coming again, because He said He was. We don't live in fear of that event. We live in hope because that Second Coming isn't about anything but goodness: God's goodness reigning supreme, reconciling, healing, and remaking the world into His image — the way it was always supposed to be.

Remember...

- God dwells in eternity, where there is no beginning and no end. We don't. That means our lives on earth, and the very earth itself, will come to an end.

- There is little that we know about the end of the world except what God reveals through Scripture, and even that isn't much. He tells us that the world will end, that evil will be destroyed, that we will be judged, and the universe will be reconciled into a "new creation and a new earth."

- Any details beyond that are speculation into a reality that our limited human minds can't possibly comprehend yet, or misreadings of Scripture.

CHAPTER 8

I've Always Wondered...

... Was Jesus Really God?

SUPPOSE YOU KNEW A GUY at school — a nice guy, to be sure, who does his homework and never mouths off to a teacher and has even shared his jalapeno-cream-cheese-mocha-flavored chips with you on occasion.

As you've gotten to know this nice guy, though, you've started to wonder about him a little bit. Why?

Because this guy is claiming to be God.

Well, he doesn't come right out and say it, but when you listen carefully to his words, there's no denying that that seems to be his basic point.

For example, just last Friday, there were these two girls crying in the hall. (Sophomores, of course. Whenever you see a girl crying in a school hallway, you can bet she's a sophomore. Same when a boy is sitting in the office for fighting. Guaranteed.) Why were they crying? Oh, because they'd had a big fight, and one had accused the other of stealing her necklace, and the other one had denied it and called her something that sounds a lot like "witch," and it was just a big mess.

So this nice guy walks by, listens to the girls recount their mutual sins, and walks away, but not before dropping a bomb himself:

"Your sins are forgiven."

And yes, you're absolutely sure that's what he said.

There have been other things, too. He's been heard to say that he and "the father" are one. Not to speak of the fact that when he was explaining why he didn't go to church, he said something like, "It's okay. I'm in charge of the Sabbath, anyway."

What, exactly, would you say about this guy?

Would you say, perhaps, that he just might be a little crazy?

And if you didn't say that, wouldn't you be tempted to suggest that this guy was nothing but a pathological liar and, because of that, perhaps not such a nice guy?

After all, if he's not God, then he must be one of those two things, right? And he can't just be a simple nice person whom everyone in school should revere as a prophet. There's really no in between, if you think about it.

Lord, Liar, or Lunatic. Those are your basic choices.

With Jesus, I mean, in case you haven't caught my drift yet.

It might seem fairly simple to just lean back in your chair, take a deep breath and say, so wisely, "Yeah, Jesus was a good guy. Anyone can tell that from what He said and did. The world would be a much

better place if everyone followed His teaching, that's for sure. But God? Nah. Couldn't be."

He certainly was a good guy. You can't disagree with that. There's not a word in this book so far that would contradict that perception. Jesus talked about love, healed the sick, defended the poor, cared for the outcast. Who but a good guy does stuff like that?

And why is it even necessary to take the next step, the step Christians insist on taking, anyway? Why not be content with Jesus the Inspiration, Jesus the Teacher, or Jesus the Spiritual Role Model?

Because the evidence won't let us walk away, that's why.

Forget the Resurrection — not permanently, of course, but just for a few minutes. Let's talk about the issue of Jesus' divinity without appealing to that for the moment.

Go back to the original question: If Jesus wasn't divine, if He wasn't God's Son, what was He?

The great Christian writer C.S. Lewis came up with a very famous answer to that question, one of the best. He said, judging from the evidence of the Gospels, that if Jesus wasn't God, then He was one of two things:

He was either a liar or a lunatic.

Let's take them one at a time.

Jesus, of course, didn't walk around introducing Himself by saying, "Hey there, I'm Jesus, but you can call me Son of God." In fact there are times in which He seemed to actually discourage people from talking about Him that way.

But there are other times in which it's clear that Jesus, while He doesn't often come right out and say it, pretty clearly hints at a unique identity:

⤷ When Jesus heals or drives out demons, He never appeals to any greater authority to do so. He never says anything like, "In the name of God, I heal you." No — Jesus' power to do that

... Was Jesus Really God? 103

kind of good, it seems, doesn't come from any external source. It comes from within.

⮌ Jesus declares that people's sins are forgiven. As we've said before, that's God's work (Mark 2:5-12).

⮌ Jesus claims authority over the Sabbath, and by extension, the Law (Luke 6:1-5).

⮌ Jesus says that He and the Father are one (John 10:30).

⮌ Finally, as John records it, Jesus makes the most astonishing statement of all:

Amen, amen, I say to you, before Abraham came to be, I AM. (John 8:58)

Do you know what this means? Way back in the book of Exodus, God revealed His name to Moses:

I am who am. (Exodus 3:14)

In other words, God is the absolute Being, upon whom all the rest of existence is dependent. This is the source of "Yahweh," the name of God the Jews were forbidden to utter aloud or even write down, because in the ancient world, being able to name something was an indication of having power over that thing, and of course, no one has power over God.

So Jesus is certainly saying a lot in those few words. He's saying that He, a man standing there talking to a bunch of Pharisees in first-century Judea, existed before Abraham. Even worse, He's blaspheming just by saying God's name. Worst of all, of course, He's applying that name to Himself.

No wonder, as John records, His listeners responded by picking up stones to throw at Him. No wonder.

So no, Jesus didn't make His identity an explicit issue, nor did He preach about it. But in everything He said and did, He made it clear,

not only that He had a uniquely intimate relationship with God, but that in some mysterious way, He actually shared God's identity.

This, quite simply, is what Jesus said. This is how He acted — healing people, forgiving their sins, and approaching the Law as if He had power over every bit of it: over nature, over sin, and even over religion.

Now, if He *wasn't* God, and He did and said all of these things, what does that make Him?

It makes Him either a liar or a bit off in the head.

If He's either of those, then He can't be that other thing you really hoped He'd be if not God: He can't be a good man.

Why? Because "good men" who are worth emulating and worth listening to don't lie. They certainly don't base their entire public lives on a humongous lie concerning their very identity.

The other alternative is that the guy was just off His rocker. He, like many other tragically insane people through history, had profound delusions of grandeur. Kind of sad, really, when you think about it.

But there are problems with that, too. We don't want to engage in stereotypes here, and we're certainly not going to mock anyone, either, but we have to be honest, too.

Did Jesus act like an insane person?

Sure, there are levels of delusion, and people with slight delusions can be highly functional, and medication can work blessings and wonders. But when you read the Gospels, does the Jesus you read about seem to be out of control in the least? Does He seem to be disturbed in any way?

No, He doesn't. But if He was, and if His statements about His own identity were, indeed, the fruit of delusion, then there goes your "Good man, prophet" argument out the window, just as quickly as it did with the liar hypothesis.

So where does that leave us?

Logically speaking, and with a clear look at the record we're left with, it's obvious we can't just blow Jesus off by saying "He was a good man." Good men don't mislead people into thinking they're the Messiah, and sane good men don't take God's unutterable name, utter it, and apply it to themselves.

Just doesn't happen.

So, by process of elimination, we're left with one conclusion that will either delight or distress us, depending on our point of view:

Jesus was Lord.

He was who He said He was. He didn't lie, and He wasn't deluded.

> The idea of a great moral teacher saying what Christ said is out of the question. In my opinion, the only person who can say that sort of thing is either God or a complete lunatic suffering from that form of delusion which undermines the whole mind of a man ... We may note in passing that He was never regarded as a mere moral teacher. He did not produce that effect on any of the people who actually met Him. He produced mainly three effects — Hatred — Terror — Adoration. There was no trace of people expressing mild approval.
> — C.S. Lewis, "What are We to Make of Jesus Christ," *God in the Dock*

There's other evidence for Jesus' divinity, of course. The miracles and His Resurrection would make the top of that list.

Also on the list, as we've said in other contexts throughout this book, is the witness of the apostles themselves, and what happened as a result of it: something called the Church.

No, they didn't get it right away — their obtuseness and Jesus' reaction to it is actually kind of funny sometimes, as well as heartening to the rest of us. But after they received the Spirit Jesus promised at Pentecost (oh yes — might that not be another bit of evidence?), it all fit together, at last — they got His teaching. They understood who He was and why He'd been among them. And they went out and told other people about it.

And note — it wasn't years later when they started doing this. It was *right away*. Right away, when memories of the crucified Jesus, the guy who blasphemed God and threatened the stability of the Empire, were still fresh. Right away, when their own lives were still in danger.

Yes, they started preaching this message immediately and fearlessly: *Jesus is Lord.*

Not "was," but "is" — making it pretty clear that their experience had revealed to them that Jesus was still alive.

Not "is a great teacher" or "is a fabulous role model" or even "is a prophet for our times." No, is *Lord*, meaning that Jesus reigns. He's in charge. He's (gulp) God.

If you want to test all of these pieces of evidence for yourself, be my guest. Pick up that Bible that's sitting by your side and open it to the middle of one of the Gospels. Start reading about this guy Jesus as if you've never heard of Him before, as if His words were totally unfamiliar to you, and as if He's nothing more than another human being like yourself. I guarantee that if you do this, you'll finish reading, look up, and think one of three things:

"This guy was crazy."

"This guy told some pretty far-fetched stories."

Or:

"Truly, this guy was the Son of God."

Remember...

- Jesus was certainly all the things the world says He was: a good teacher, a good man, and a prophet. He was, however, something more: He was fully divine.

- He forgave sins, which only God can do.

- He claimed authority over the Sabbath and the entire Law

- He said He and the Father were "one."

- If Jesus were not God, as He claimed, He would then be a liar or deluded, and in neither case would we be able to say He was a "good man."

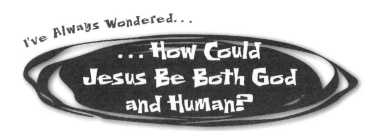

CHAPTER 9

I've Always Wondered...

... How Could Jesus Be Both God and Human?

YOU ARE SUCH AN AMAZING MYSTERY, my friend.

Please don't be insulted — I mean it in a good way, really.

If you think about it for a minute, you'll no doubt agree with me.

It's a mystery how that teeny-tiny embryo, that red little newborn baby squinting out from under that little knit cap the hospital gives out, the very cool guy you are now, and the slowly-moving, yet content grandfather of twelve that you're going to be, are one and the same person.

It's a mystery how you and your best friend can just lock eyes from across the room during history class and know *exactly* what the other is thinking.

It's a mystery how so much knowledge can be crammed in your brain, even though, if the scientists are right, you're only using about ten percent of that brain.

It's a mystery how you can sit in front of a blank piece of paper, a blinking computer screen, a piano, or a formless lump of clay, and you can take the pictures, ideas, and words in your mind and create something completely unique and new.

It's a mystery how all of this — your thoughts, emotions, and creativity, not to speak of your spirituality — are somehow welded to and woven with a physical body.

It's a mystery how you — a person taking up a particular piece of space in a particular point in time — can be comforted in the dark of night by the Creator of the whole universe.

You see, mystery is not a bad thing, even though the term's sometimes used that way. People accuse Christians of falling back on the term "mystery" as somewhat of a cop-out in these oh-so-rational times when nothing's considered "true" unless it can be subjected to the scientific method and explained with an equation.

But to say something is a mystery isn't a cop-out at all. It's just the way things are. We don't use the term to dissuade you from investigating a concept that you might find to be falsehood. We just use it to describe.

When we say that certain matters — a lot, if you want to know the truth — in religion and the rest of life fall under the realm of "mystery," what we're saying is that there is stuff that is beyond the capacity of our limited intellects to fully understand and express.

Take God. If God is who we say He is, He is, without doubt, mystery. There's no way that human minds — even if we were using more than a fraction of our brain power after all — could comprehend the Creator of the universe. If we could, He wouldn't be God at all, then, would He?

But as you undoubtedly saw at the very beginning of this chapter, God isn't the only aspect of life that's mysterious. There are lots of aspects of your existence that fall under that category as well. We listed some of them above, but they all come down to one most mysterious question of all: Why are you here instead of not here?

What scientist could ever answer that question, or the even bigger question of why there is *something* rather than *nothing* in the first place?

Jesus

Oh yes, I know — this is a book about Jesus, not you. But before we talk about this most vexing, perplexing question of Jesus' identity, it's good to be reminded that the mystery of Jesus' identity, while profound, is just a little bit similar to the mystery of your own.

You're wondering how in the world the Creator of the universe, who's omnipotent and omnipresent, can be enfleshed in a helpless baby. It's an astounding reality to contemplate, isn't it? But it's also astounding that *any* spiritual entity, capable of thought, creativity and eternal life, can be enfleshed in *any* helpless baby. In a way, you can see the Incarnation as the perfection of what God did in human beings from the beginning: meshing flesh and spirit, mortality and immortality.

> Just as every human being is one person, that is, a rational soul and body, so, too, is Christ one Person, the Word and man.
> — St. Augustine, *Enchiridion*

That's really the point here. It's important that you be able to see that Jesus' presence in time and space is the defining moment in human history, that it's radical, that it shines a new, transforming light on everything.

But it's also important for you to see that this invasion, as C.S. Lewis puts it when he talks about miracles, isn't an alien invasion. It doesn't introduce anything that's out of sync with the rest of creation. Rather, it completes it — it's a friendly invasion. God come to earth is the completion of what God started.

It ties all the loose threads of creation together and makes sense of all the paradoxes: death and life, sin and forgiveness, suffering and glory.

The mystery of God becoming one with human flesh isn't that much more mysterious than the fact that you, mortal being, just might live forever.

Jesus' Identity

Jesus was one person with two natures: divine and human.

He was *fully* human and *fully* divine, too. Let's figure out what that means, and as is the case with most complicated matters, it's sometimes more helpful to point out what the idea *doesn't* mean first.

It doesn't mean Jesus was divided in half. He didn't act like God one minute and a human being the next. He didn't have a switch on His back — well, that would have been hard to reach — on His arm, then, that He could flip to turn His divinity on and off.

Jesus wasn't a ghost running around, a spirit who could fool people into thinking He had a real body. He had a real, totally human body, from head to toe.

Jesus wasn't a really amazing angel or a human being with superpowers, or God's trusty assistant. He was God. The Supreme Being. I Am Who Am.

Jesus wasn't born a human being and given His divinity later when He was baptized or when He rose from the dead. He was who He was from the beginning.

I've Always Wondered . . .

Sure, we'd like to know how it all worked together, how eternity could co-exist within a mortal body, how omniscience could toddle around the house in Nazareth learning how to talk, and how omnipresence works with a baby nursing at His mother's breast.

But we can't, and we're just going to have to accept the mystery. Our own human nature is so much of a mystery, we shouldn't be surprised that Jesus' is, too.

Not that people haven't tried to explain it, of course, as the whole issue is just too intriguing to drop.

What bugs people (and maybe you, too), is that while Jesus was more knowledgeable than even the teachers of the Law at a young age (remember the story about the Temple when He was twelve?), in general, He didn't seem to stand out as some freakish, all-knowing fellow during His younger years.

He may have confounded everyone He met during His public ministry, but He seems to have kept a normal, rather low profile while he was growing up.

The evangelists record various comments from the citizens of Nazareth and Galilee indicating that they thought of Jesus as little more than "the carpenter's son," and they're startled that He ended up pointing to Himself as the fulfillment of a prophecy, no less:

> And all spoke highly of Him and were amazed at the gracious words that came from His mouth. They also asked, "Isn't this the son of Joseph?"
>
> (LUKE 4:22)

It's as if you'd never picked up a basketball in your life and all of a sudden your neighbors saw you on television, playing in the NBA. "Who is this?" they'd wonder, "Is this not the kid who sat in his room for ten years straight playing video games? How could this come to be?"

In other words, Jesus didn't seem to strike anyone as anything but a normal guy while He was growing up, and Luke even ends the story of the boy Jesus in the Temple by observing,

> *And Jesus advanced [in] wisdom and age and favor before*
> *God and man.* (LUKE 2:52)

How, you wonder, could Jesus "grow in wisdom" if He was the omniscient God? How could be seriously tempted? And why did He pray?

Sorry to say, but it's a mystery. Oh, I could spend a lot of pages outlining various theories that have been developed over the centuries, but they're really only that: theories. Interesting. Intriguing. Ultimately not of much use.

For you see, we're back at another place where we just have to trust God. If God thought it was important for us to understand precisely how Jesus' divine and human nature interacted, He'd have told us. But He didn't, did He?

So what is it we're supposed to get out of this Jesus business? If we're not supposed to get the internal workings of the Divine Mind, what is it about Jesus, the Incarnation of God in human flesh, that we're supposed to see?

How about this:

Love.

The philosophical questions are fascinating, but as you've figured out, they're unanswerable. We know that God's omniscient, omnipresent, and omnipotent, and we know that Jesus is God, no doubt about it, so we think sometimes that the way to respond to those truths is to twist and turn all the "omni's" so they fit inside the baby, and when we figure out how they fit, we'll have found a reason to believe.

When we do that, though, we've got it completely backwards.

After all, we're talking about knowing a person here, and that is not at all how we get to know persons — we shouldn't, anyway.

If you see a baby, you don't study it, thinking about what it *should*

be and what human nature is all about and how that baby manifests intellect, will, creativity, and love.

What would you get if you did that anyway? A lot of drool on your shirt, probably.

No, what you do is you get to know the baby. Over time, you let the baby reveal who she is. You watch what the baby does and as she grows, you listen to what she says.

Then you see who she is, not because you've defined her, but because she's told you who she is.

That is exactly what we should do with Jesus, too.

We look at Jesus — baby, young person, and adult — accepting the witness of the apostles who died for their conviction that this fully human person was also Lord, and we watch and listen. What do we learn about this Lord, our God, when we do that?

We learn that God is love. We learn that He is endlessly forgiving. We learn that He wants the world to return to its original beauty and wholeness, and given the opening we offer through faith, He makes it happen. We learn that He will do anything and everything — even submit to death — because He loves us so much.

Do you see that this is why, in the first chapter of John's Gospel, Jesus is called the "Word?" He's called that because God speaks through Him. And what's the best response to a Word? To talk over it? To tell it what it means?

No, the only response to a Word is to listen.

So yes, what we have here is a mystery. But you should have figured out by now that the most wonderful, important things in life are always — every time — mysterious. The love your parents have for you despite how unappreciative you are of them. The astonishing things of unending variety that human beings can do with paints, musical notes, and words. The way you came into existence.

It's all mystery, and the most boring thing in the world is to sit around and try to analyze the mystery instead of enjoying it, appreciating it, and immersing yourself in it.

So when you think about the mystery of Jesus' Incarnation, it's really a waste of time to play with those picky questions. The question of "how" is intriguing, but the question of "why" is much better, and better yet, the answer's all over the place, which is something you can't say for "how."

> For God so loved the world that he gave his only Son, so that everyone who believes in him might not perish but might have eternal life. (JOHN 3:16)

Remember . . .

- Jesus is one person with two natures: divine and human. He is fully divine and fully human. How the two natures interacted while Jesus was on earth is a mystery.

- The belief that Jesus is fully divine and fully human was part of the earliest Christian preaching, as the apostles declared, "Jesus Christ is Lord" (Phillipians 2:11).

- As the centuries passed, explanations of Jesus' dual nature became more detailed and explicit, but those doctrinal explanations are built on the clear witness of Jesus' words and actions, His Resurrection, and the experience of the apostles.

- When we listen to Jesus, we learn who God is.

CHAPTER 10

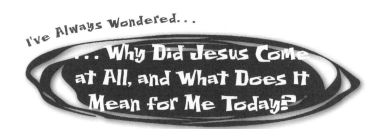

BACK IN THE DAY, people got pretty excited about Jesus.

No doubt about it: Those guys named Peter, James, John, and eight more of their best friends couldn't keep quiet about Jesus.

When it finally all made sense to them — after the Crucifixion, after the Resurrection and Ascension and then after the Spirit came to them at Pentecost — they saw no other way to live their lives but for Jesus.

And that's just what they did.

We've hammered home this point quite a bit throughout the past hundred or so pages, and now it's time to really strike it hard:

The people who knew Jesus personally gave every inch of their being, every second of their lives to sharing the Good News about Him:

He'd been killed, but He was still alive.

He is Lord.

Without Him, the world would be a completely different place.

Flash forward about two thousand years.

So?

What's your response?

Oh, you don't get it, do you? See, when the apostles spread out and told everyone about Jesus, His message, His death, and His Risen Life, they weren't just talking to folks gathered in the Corinth town square or on the edge of Philippi.

I've Always Wondered . . .

They were talking to you.

Are you listening yet?

I hope by this point, you have a much, much clearer sense of who Jesus is and what He's about than you did when you started. You understand His message about love, God, and the kingdom of God. You see how this kingdom of God broke through in amazing ways whenever Jesus performed a miracle. You see, a little better at least, what we mean when we say Jesus died for us. You get the Resurrection, and see how strong the evidence for it is.

You see how clear it is, through the simple evidence of the Gospels, that what the apostles said from the beginning is true: Jesus is Lord.

And maybe you've not only seen this stuff, maybe you've heard something, too.

Maybe you've heard the voice of Jesus, calling:

Come, follow me.

What are you going to say?

Why Follow Jesus?

Because He's telling the truth, that's why.

I mean, do you really have a choice? A life-giving, joyful, love-filled choice, that is.

If all that you've read has convinced you that the Gospels are accurate records of what Jesus said, and that Jesus told the truth about God and Himself, why would you turn your back on that truth?

For you see, if you did that, what would you be turning *toward?*

Lies, I guess. And I guess you could list all of those lies, as well.

Think of all that Jesus taught and then just turn that around. Selfishness instead of love. Meaningless instead of meaning. No God instead of God.

But, you say . . . I can follow all that Jesus taught, without following Jesus, can't I?

Haven't we been through this before?

If Jesus is a truth-teller, then He's a truth-teller about everything He chooses to talk about. You can't say, "Ah yes, that guy Jesus said some very, very true things about love, so I'll think I'll live by that. But He also told some pretty huge lies about Himself, so I'll just forget that part of it."

Can't do it. Lord, Liar or Lunatic, remember?

And you really have to think very, very hard here, and answer this question honestly:

Why do you want to say no to Jesus?

What are you afraid of?

What is it you're going to lose by saying "yes?" Is it really worth keeping?

> We are half-hearted creatures, fooling about with drink and sex and ambition when infinite joy is offered us, like an ignorant child who wants to go on making mud pies in a slum because he cannot imagine what is meant by the offer of a holiday at the sea. We are far too easily pleased.
> — C.S. Lewis, *The Weight of Glory*

So you want to say "yes." Maybe you already did. Maybe you want to start taking the promises that were made for you at your baptism seriously. What is that going to mean?

You Have a Best Friend

A Christian doesn't just believe certain things, although that's important. More than that, a Christian is a person who is in relationship with God through Jesus. Every single aspect of your life is refracted through

I've Always Wondered . . .

the prism of that friendship. And that's the way you should think of it: a friendship with the One who loves you more than anyone else does, who loved you so much He created you — the amazing, unique you — on purpose, mind you. He also loved you enough to suffer terribly for you, so you wouldn't have to be constrained by sin or death anymore.

> The Son of God became a man to enable men to become sons of God.
> — C.S. Lewis, *Mere Christianity*

If that seems confining to you, think again. Sometimes our friendships can be confining and limiting, but those, we find upon reflection, aren't good friendships, and may not even be friendships at all. Think of how liberating real love is — what kind of confidence it gives you. Take that and multiply it by infinity. That's what knowing God is really and truly on your side will do for you.

It's knowing, quite frankly, that what other people think of you doesn't matter one bit. The opinions of snotty fifteen-year-old girls or obtuse seventeen-year-old boys or advertisers or even your parents don't fundamentally define who you are. What defines you is the fact that God loves you. Can you imagine the places you'll go in life if you just take that and run with it?

You Know What's Right

No more searching for you. Oh sure, you'll have to do some hard thinking, reflecting and praying along the way to discern how the words of Jesus apply to specific situations in your life, that's true.

Jesus didn't, after all, lay out precisely how to deal with the question of how much time you should spend on the computer or playing video games versus how much of the day you should give to studies or just enjoying life as it really is, rather than how a screen presents it. He didn't outline a point-by-point method of coping with the strains of family life.

But you know what? The things He *did* say apply to all of those situations, and if you can't figure out exactly how, you have two more ways to help you figure it out: You have the wisdom of the Church, the Body of Christ on earth, and you have Jesus present to you in a personal way, every time you pray, and especially every time you lay all your questions and problems out in His Presence in the Eucharist.

He's alive, remember? We keep coming back to that over and over again. Being a Christian doesn't just mean living according to certain standards. It means being in a living relationship with Him every minute of every day.

> Christianity is more than a doctrine; it is Christ Himself living in those whom He has united to Himself in One Mystical Body.
> — Thomas Merton, *The Living Bread*

There may be a million voices out there trying to tell you what the meaning of life is, competing for your attention, your loyalty, not to speak of your dollars, but that's not really anything you have to worry

about anymore. Jesus has spoken, and just as importantly, Jesus lives within you, guiding you, loving you, and strengthening you.

So you know:

- ⏤ You're created and loved by God.
- ⏤ When you turn from God and God's love, it's not the end. You can be forgiven and empowered not to make the same mistake next time.
- ⏤ You're called to bring God's love into other people's lives.
- ⏤ Your life is not lived for yourself, but for others. You'll have to sacrifice, but so be it. Jesus leads the way.
- ⏤ God isn't far away. You speak to Him many times a day in prayer, and you gather with others on Sunday to worship, just as the early Christians did from the beginning.
- ⏤ Your death will only be a step toward eternal life.

Before We Say Goodbye

So there you are. You began this book knowing that Jesus had some kind of pull on you that no other figure, past or present, does. But you couldn't quite put your finger on it, and for sure, you were a little uncertain how to explain it to nonbelievers.

I hope this helped!

Moreover, I hope that all of these words have worked to clear away some of those doubts and questions you had, so you can make space in your heart for something far, far more important:

The loving presence of Jesus, vibrant, strong, and alive.

He's here, you know. He's speaking the same words of forgiveness He spoke to the woman caught in adultery, to you in your heart and very powerfully in the Sacrament of Reconciliation.

He's invited you to be in loving friendship with Him at your baptism and at your confirmation.

Christ has no body now on earth but yours,
no hands but yours, no feet but yours,
Yours are the eyes through which is to look out
Christ's compassion to the world;
Yours are the feet with which he is to go about
  doing good;
Yours are the hands with which he is to bless
  men now.
                                — St. Teresa of Avila

And every time you're in His presence in Eucharist . . . well, you're with Him. The same Jesus who healed, forgave, and loved without boundaries two thousand years ago is right there, offering you that very same love that assures you that you are incredibly precious, and because you are so loved, you can go out and share that same love with every person you meet.

Some people like to present Christianity as a confining way of life. You see that's not so. It's not confining to live in God's love. It's the most liberating thing in the world.

Finally, because of Jesus, you know exactly who you are, and nothing — not possessions, not your bad habits, not your past, not your not temptation, not sin, and not even death — can have any power over you. It's joy you'll have for the rest of your life on earth, then through eternity.

How can you say anything but "Yes" to that?

> If God is for us, who can be against us? He who did not spare his own Son but handed him over for us all, how will he not also give us everything else along with him? . . . What will separate us from the love of Christ? Will anguish, or distress, or persecution, or famine, or nakedness, or peril, or the sword? . . . No, in all these things we conquer overwhelmingly through him who loved us. For I

am convinced that neither death, nor life, nor angels, nor principalities, nor present things, nor future things, nor powers, nor height, nor depth, nor any other creature will be able to separate us from the love of God in Christ Jesus our Lord. — ROMANS 8:31-32, 35, 37-39

 JESUS

PALESTINE IN THE TIME OF JESUS

TO EUROPE

N

TO EGYPT

Capernaum

Mediterranean Sea

GALILEE

Sea of Galilee

Nazareth

River Jordan

SAMARIA

Jerusalem

Bethlehem

JUDEA

Salt Sea (Dead Sea)

But I want more!

Like **Prove It! Jesus?** You'll love these other titles in the Prove It! series by Amy Welborn ...

Prove It! God

The first in the series, **Prove It! God** answers the REAL questions you have about God, evolution, good and evil, and a whole lot of other things you never hear about in religion class, in Sunday homilies, or from your parents. You have nothing to lose – but your doubts!

0-87973-396-9, (396) paper, 128 pp.

Prove It! Church

What do you say when someone tells you you're not a Christian because what your church teaches isn't in the Bible, or you worship Mary like a goddess? **Prove It! Church** gives you the answers, proving the Catholic Church belongs to Christ and *is* Christ in the world today.

0-87973-981-9, (981) paper, 160 pp.

Prove It! Prayer

You know you *should* talk to God. You know He can help. You know you should tell Him thanks once in a while, too. But where do you start? **Prove It! Prayer** describes how and why you should put a meaningful chat with God at the top of your daily to-do list.

0-87973-544-9, (544) paper, 112 pp.

ABOUT THE AUTHOR

Amy Welborn has an M.A. in religion from Vanderbilt University. She taught high school theology for nine years. Since 1994, she has been writing a syndicated column on Catholic youth for Catholic News Service and is a columnist for *Our Sunday Visitor.*

OurSundayVisitor

200 Noll Plaza / Huntington, IN 46750
1-800-348-2440 / osvbooks@osv.com / www.osv.com
Availability of books subject to change without notice.   A29BBABP

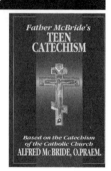